Lessons
ⁱⁿ radical
innovation

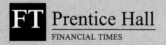

FT Prentice Hall
FINANCIAL TIMES

In an increasingly competitive world, we believe it's quality of thinking that will give you the edge – an idea that opens new doors, a technique that solves a problem, or an insight that simply makes sense of it all. The more you know, the smarter and faster you can go.

That's why we work with the best minds in business and finance to bring cutting-edge thinking and best learning practice to a global market.

Under a range of leading imprints, including *Financial Times Prentice Hall*, we create world-class print publications and electronic products bringing our readers knowledge, skills and understanding which can be applied whether studying or at work.

To find out more about our business publications, or tell us about the books you'd like to find, you can visit us at **www.business-minds.com**

For other Pearson Education publications, visit **www.pearsoned-ema.com**

Lessons

in radical

innovation

Out of the box —

straight to the bottom line

Wolfgang Grulke

with Gus Siber

 Prentice Hall
FINANCIAL TIMES

An imprint of Pearson Education

Harlow, England • London • New York • Boston • San Francisco • Toronto
Sydney • Tokyo • Singapore • Hong Kong • Seoul • Taipei • New Delhi
Cape Town • Madrid • Mexico City • Amsterdam • Munich • Paris • Milan

PEARSON EDUCATION LIMITED

Edinburgh Gate
Harlow, Essex CM20 2JE
Tel: +44 (0)1279 623623
Fax: +44 (0)1279 431059

Website: www.pearsoned.co.uk

South African edition published in 2001 by
@One Communications, PO Box 651471, Benmore 2010, South Africa

International edition first published in Great Britain in 2002

ISBN: 0 273 65948 0

British Library Cataloguing in Publication Data
A CIP catalogue record for this book is available from the British Library

10 9 8 7 6 5

Designed by Claire Brodmann Book Designs, Lichfield, Staffs.
Typeset by Pantek Arts Ltd, Maidstone, Kent.
Printed and bound in Great Britain by Biddles Ltd, King's Lynn, Norfolk

The Publishers' policy is to use paper manufactured from sustainable forests.

From Wolfgang to Terri

Magical wife, lover and closest friend

From Gus to Amanda

With love and thanks

Contents

Prologue: The map is not the territory!

Innovation has become the
economic religion of
the 21st Century, but on its own,
innovation is no longer enough to

differentiate you from "the bunch".

To thrive today, you need radical innovation.

Yes, you've heard it all before. Some crazy consultant pushing change, change, change.

Thomas Stewart, writing in his column in *Fortune* magazine, likened innovation to either a machine or a garden. If it is a machine, companies should design it, build it and manage it. If it is a garden, companies should create the conditions in which it can flourish and then let the magic occur.

What I'll try to show in this book is that it is both. Innovation requires a process, management and tools, but also bold leadership, inspiration and an open tolerant culture in which it can flourish.

But you will find that this book is not a blueprint for change. It is not a "How to" book. This is not a road map to the territory called innovation.

There is no guaranteed blueprint that can turn your successful business into an innovative business. There's no golden bullet for radical innovation.

As you may have noticed, most maps don't describe the territory very well. A map of New York City looks much the same as it did 50 years ago. Nowhere does it tell you where the pot holes or the traffic jams are. Nowhere an indication of where your radio may be stolen while you're listening to it. Nowhere does a map of Johannesburg highlight where your car may be hijacked. The only way you learn about the territory of the real world is to talk, and listen to, the survivors.

In case you're in a hurry, let me give you the conclusion of my book right here, right now.

There is no guaranteed blueprint that can turn your successful business into an innovative business. There's no golden bullet for radical innovation.

Failure. Now there's a great catalyst. Success, I'm afraid, just doesn't cut it in the innovation stakes. Successful companies appear to turn into "serial incrementalists", leaving the radical stuff to the crazy young upstarts.

What I will do is look at the practical experiences of great innovators for some clues to the things that might work in your business.

But one thing's for sure.

The more radical you go, the more likely failure will become.

It seems we have to accept a failure rate of more than 50 per cent if we want to become radical entrepreneurs. The really important thing is not to give up. To learn the lessons of failure, to apply them, to continue taking risks, to continue innovating.

But why subject ourselves and our businesses to this kind of risk?

I am a passionate scribbler. Open white space beckons me! When I communicate, I tend to communicate actively, creating images and pictures, spontaneously, at random, on walls, flip charts, or any other available surface.

With that in mind, I have left many of the left-hand pages of this book essentially "blank". The future itself is a blank slate, waiting to be filled in by you and you alone. The blank pages in this book are a perfect metaphor for this way of thinking. Unable to resist the temptation, I've used some of the blank spaces to draw a few images of my own for you. I hope they'll illustrate the text in a more conceptual way. Sometimes my editor has taken the liberty of adding a quote from the text.

Often the page has been intentionally left blank – just for you.

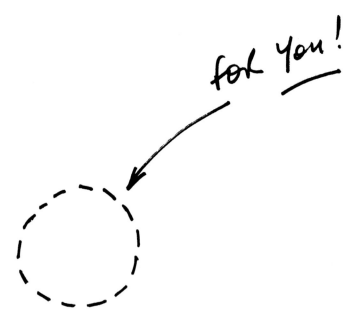

Take a pen or pencil. Do it now. Add some graffiti yourself. Do some white-space thinking! Write down your expectations of this book and re-visit them later. Air your views, if only to re-state the ideas in the book, in ways more relevant to you or your business.

For you too, I hope this book will become your "work in progress".

The consequences of a lack of innovation are severe. They are directly reflected in economic performance. Think of the South African example. In the 1960s, South Africa represented 6 per cent of world GDP. Today that figure is less than 0.5 per cent, but year-on-year the South African economy has never shrunk. South Africa has simply been out-innovated by other nations who saw the signs and acted fast.

Today half of America's economic growth comes from products that barely existed a decade ago! The degree to which this happens has become a key measure of national success.

Innovation has become the economic religion of the 21st Century, but it's no longer enough to differentiate you from "the bunch". To thrive today, you need radical innovation. That's what this book is really about. It's about real people like you and me. People who took risks and set themselves outrageous goals, against almost impossible odds.

These are just some of the individuals and corporations leading the charge into the future.

Included here are people and companies with whom I have shared a common destiny. We have often worked and debated into the early hours, way beyond the common sense of sleep.

Here are the stories of those people who have shared my passion for the future, who were prepared to share their ideas and create magic in the process. Sheer magic for their staff, investors, customers and clients.

Through thought leadership and
breakthrough implementation
they brought radical
innovation to life.

In the end, these people surprised not only their markets and competitors. Often, they surprised themselves with the degree of innovation they achieved. These are people who set outrageous goals that they themselves considered tough to achieve.

Then they went out and surpassed these goals.
Are you ready to do the same?

Following the passionate feedback we received from readers of my previous book, *Ten Lessons from the Future*, this book has again been designed to encourage you to read *actively*.

Most of the books in my collection have margins covered in comments and sketches. I don't just read books. I actively interact with them! I encourage you to do the same with this book.

Finally, words of thanks to those without whom this book would not have been possible.

Firstly to Terri, who was my companion on so many of the trips that led to this book. She challenged my thinking all along the way and ensured that we learnt from everyone and everything we encountered. The thinking is clearer because of her.

For constant inspiration and a powerful pull into the future, I must thank my partners and friends in the FutureWorld Network of Gurus. In much of the work we do, we have become one at heart. And hopefully we are all the better for it.

In this work, my role as a Director of the Deloitte and Touche global Innovation Board has given me a sounding board and a laboratory for new thinking. Direct access to its client companies proved invaluable and certainly helped mirror some of our own lessons in radical innovation.

My editor, Gus Silber, has once again done sterling work in pulling all the "stuff" together and turning it into what you see between these pages. He has become a vital partner in weaving these stories of innovation.

I hope that these inspirational innovators will encourage you to be positive, take risks and do amazing things.

From all of us, and all of me, to all of you – enjoy being radical.

Choose a radical future – and thrive in it!

Wolfgang Grulke

The catalysts of radical innovation

The drivers of quantum change

Let's talk about words. Let's begin with one of the most powerful words of all...

"Innovation".

It's fascinating how the word "innovation" has become such a positive concept. Words like "invention" and "evolution" are much less sought after to describe major achievements.

When someone describes your business as "innovative" you feel great. But if they call you "inventive" the compliment seems somewhat dubious – as if your real skill is for making things up.

If someone says that your business is "evolving", the comment will probably leave you stone cold! It's interesting how the concept of "evolution" has become so linked to Darwin's theories. It certainly does not, at first, appear to be relevant within the context of an innovative business.

And how often do we not bandy about the word "technology" as one of the key change agents – without so much as a thought for what the word means.

Innovation. Invention. Evolution. Technology. These four words embody powerful concepts, but they are words that are much misunderstood.

When we hear the word "evolution", our first thoughts turn to Charles Darwin and the evolution of species. Let's start by exploring a few aspects of this "evolution" and see what lessons we might learn in terms of innovation.

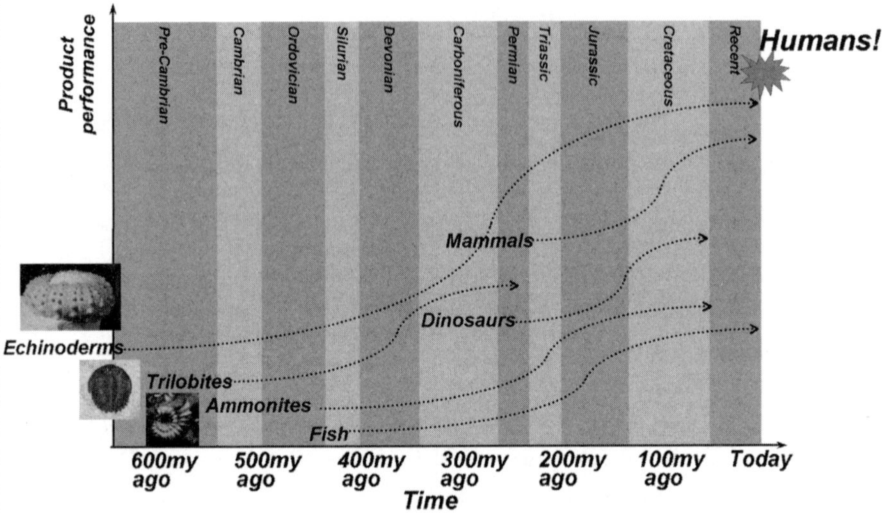
Product performance
Pre-Cambrian
Cambrian
Ordovician
Silurian
Devonian
Carboniferous
Permian
Triassic
Jurassic
Cretaceous
Recent
Humans!
Mammals
Dinosaurs
Echinoderms
Trilobites
Ammonites
Fish
600my ago
500my ago
400my ago
300my ago
200my ago
100my ago
Today
Time

The history of life on this planet commenced around 3.5 billion years ago with the emergence of the first proteins and bacteria. The first living communities emerged shortly thereafter – simple algae called *stromatolites* – the first living organisms to produce oxygen through photosynthesis.

Photosynthesis literally changed the balance of life...but it took 1 billion years for enough oxygen to accumulate in the atmosphere and complex cell structures to evolve. For the next 3 billion years all life forms would be aquatic.

Seven hundred million years ago the first animals emerged: jellyfish and echinoderms – sea stars, sea urchins and sea cucumbers with their typical five-sided symmetry.

Four hundred million years ago, the first animals ventured onto land. The amphibians. Two hundred million years ago, new species of reptiles, the dinosaurs, took centre stage.

Then, quite suddenly in geological time, about 65 million years ago, the great mass extinction event happened. No one can quite agree exactly what happened, since obviously no one was there. But it seems as if a massive meteorite, hitting what is now the Caribbean just off Mexico, might have been the catalyst.

In any case, in a relatively short time, all dinosaurs, together with a half of all animal species on land and in the sea, simply disappeared.

Clearly life on earth recovered. This was the dawn of the age of mammals. Life evolved in many strange and wonderful ways.

By the time man arrived, the echinoderms had already inhabited the earth for almost 700 million years. Echinoderms are a spectacular example of evolutionary innovation. Take any sea star from any rock pool off any shore anywhere in the world. Turn it upside down. You will see the result of hundreds of millions of years of evolutionary innovation. A mass of specialized tube feet, highly evolved and highly successful.

Our own ancestors emerged 4 million years ago, while modern humans, *Homo sapiens sapiens*, emerged just 100,000 years ago.

evolution

1. The process of disengaging from an exisiting envelope

2. Developing from a rudimentary to a complete state

3. The hypothesis that the embryo contains the rudiments of all parts of the future organism

4. The origin of species as a process of development from earlier forms

We've been around just 100 millennia, a very short space of time in cosmic terms. What we've achieved has been nothing short of astounding. This is radical stuff.

Why, with a head start of more than 600 million years have the echinoderms not developed an economic infrastructure? Why have they not invaded land? Why is there no echinoderm stock market?

What made the difference? Why this sudden spurt of radical innovation?

From the first hand axe carved out of brittle flint to the rise of the personal computer, from the printing press to television...technology has made the difference. Our ability to use tools to our advantage changed the balance of power on the planet.

By comparison to what came before, this is not evolutionary innovation.

The history of human development is a history punctuated by radical innovation.

Now take a look at the dictionary definitions of these catalysts of creative change: evolution, invention, innovation and technology.

You'll see that the primary meaning of *evolution* is not that associated with Darwinian evolution – that aspect was added to the original meanings subsequent to Darwin's discoveries.

How exciting the first three meanings are in the context of business innovation!

invention

1. The action of finding or discovering

2. Contrivance of a new method

innovation

1. The action of innovating

2. The change into something new

3. The introduction of novelties

4. The alteration of what is established

technology

The practice or application of any of the applied sciences
for practical value or industrial use

If we look at the meaning of the word "invention", it's no wonder that we don't want to be called "inventive" when we do something really innovative.

And what do our dictionaries say about *innovation*?

What's interesting about *innovation* and *invention*, is how mundane their definitions really are. By comparison, *evolution* sets the mind racing.

Breaking out of the envelope, creating new paradigms. What particularly excites me is the concept that the embryo contains all the rudiments of the future organism.

We already have inside us all

the building blocks of what

we will be in future.

You can choose your own future.

This is what it really comes down to. The only difference between failure and success is attitude.

Oh, and our willingness to use the technology of the day. But, what exactly is technology?

Whenever I ask an audience that question, they're quick to give me examples of such everyday devices as cellphones, TVs, PCs, and the wheel. But, are these really examples of technology?

The answer is "No!" Although in modern usage the term "technology" has come to represent all these physical devices, the true meaning of the word is different.

You see, cellphones, TVs, PCs, and the wheel are just some of the tools that helped speed our evolution.

entrepreneur

"An entrepreneur constantly shifts economic resources into areas of higher productivity and greater yield."

Jean-Baptiste Say, 1800

Technology really refers to the application of tools. What we do with tools is technology.

Surprised?

Just think about it. If you accept the above definitions, who has responsibility for technology in an organization? Clearly not the IT department. They are responsible for the tools.

The gardener is not just responsible for the shovel and rake, the gardener is responsible for the use of the tools and for adding value.

In business, technology is everyone's responsibility.

And seeing that technology has proven itself to be core to human (and business) development, anyone who doesn't get it is clearly not going to be an innovator.

And what do we call people who innovate with technology? Often we call them entrepreneurs. So what exactly is an entrepreneur? The most powerful definition I could find was one dating from the beginning of the 19th Century (see opposite).

This may be obvious to you, after reading it. The only word that may surprise here is *constantly*. The implication is that if you do it once or twice, that doesn't make you an entrepreneur. It has to be a constant continuous process.

An entrepreneur is someone who is constantly dissatisfied with the status quo.

It can be hell to have entrepreneurs working for you. No matter how well you are doing, they will always believe that things can be radically different. There is never any time to rest on your laurels. "C'mon, let's just let things settle down here," you say. Entrepreneurs are eternally impatient and unreasonable people.

Imagine having a whole team of them working for you.

technology

The marketing, investment and managerial processes
by which an organization transforms
labour, capital, materials and information
into products and services of greater value

innovation

Refers to a change in one of these "technologies"

disruptive technology

Change that topples industry leaders

Clayton Christensen, the Harvard author of the classic *The Innovator's Dilemma*, also adds some more recent perspectives to the definition of these terms – this time from a pure business perspective and in the context of his pet theme – disruptive technologies. Clayton's definition of *technology* implies that a new technology can be nothing more than an idea – anything that creates a change to the way you do business. Tools and technology are not a prerequisite to innovation.

Suddenly, for him, the definition of *innovation* becomes a very obvious, yet bland, matter. *Innovation* simply becomes a change in one of these *technologies*. When this change comes close to being *radical* then often a disruptive technology is involved. In Clayton's terminology a disruptive technology is one that always topples the industry leader.

An example of disruptive technology might be the use of the cellphone. The cellphone itself is the *tool* (remember!); what we do with it is the *technology* that topples industry leaders – in this case the old telecommunications monopolies.

This insight into the true meaning of *technology* is analogous to "knowledge and the individual". You are not what you *know*, you are what you *do*!

Tools are what you *have*.

Technology is what you *do* with those tools!

Grulke: "You are what you do!"

Radical innovation – The bottom line

innovation
plus technology
plus an entrepreneur

= A MASSIVELY DISRUPTIVE COCKTAIL

Having spent some time analyzing the basic terminology of creative change, let me define what I mean by radical innovation: innovation plus technology plus an entrepreneur equals a massively disruptive cocktail. This is what I call radical innovation.

Radical innovation always...

...breaks the mould. The current envelope cannot contain the new innovation paradigm. People ask "What are they up to?", "Are they mad?", "Do they understand this industry?" Only after the radical new idea succeeds do the old players suddenly understand the new paradigm. They "get it" from their defecting customers.

...gives significantly better returns. There is almost an order of magnitude difference in long-term returns on radical innovation – 50–60 per cent per annum returns versus the typical 10–20 per cent per annum returns on evolutionary innovation. Companies that budget incrementally, asking their divisions to all deliver 10–20 per cent per annum growth already are defining their future to be incremental. Given that mental model, few managers in the corporate hierarchy will step out of line and do something radical. This is strategy by default.

...establishes the future norm. After a new radical innovation is introduced to the market nothing will ever be the same again. No competitor can dare to enter the market with a pre-radical approach or technology. The consumer simply won't buy it.

...attracts venture capital like bees to honey. Venture capitalists, by their very nature, look for radical returns. Evolutionary ideas and products seldom attract the same level of attention, no matter how low the risk.

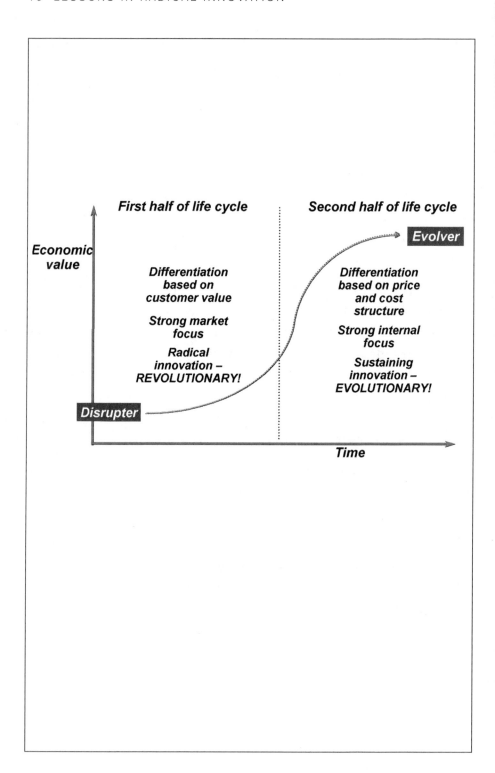

Cycles big and small

Everything in life goes through cycles of one sort or another. You can see them in the motions of the planets, the seasons and fashion. You see them in innovation, economics, products and businesses. All of them go through cycles of varying lengths.

The small cycles – business cycles

In the first half of the life cycle, all business thinking is based on customers and their needs. Products and businesses are based on whatever can add value to these customers. In the second half of the life cycle, successful companies attract many "me too" competitors who can only differentiate themselves in existing markets by cutting the price.

At this stage of the cycle, products become increasingly commoditized. Market differentiation is based increasingly on price, resulting in massive focus on costs and operational efficiencies, especially among the market leaders that established these markets. At this stage, the focus of the market leader becomes primarily internal, and innovation becomes incremental and evolutionary. The aim is to constantly improve product functionality and cost structures. It is, in fact, the new entrants price-cutting strategies that force the market leader into the efficiency spiral and its accompanying internal focus.

In the second half of the business life cycle, companies that were initially considered massive disrupters eventually succumb to the pressures of the second half of the life cycle and became evolvers. You've gone from having a powerful market focus to suffering from organizational vertigo.

This is where the *organization* becomes more important than the *business* – in the words of Stan Davis, the organizational tail starts wagging the business dog.

In fact these are two conflicting market paradigms. Which kind of organization would YOU choose to do business with? Which business model will win the soul of the customer? No contest…

Radical innovation
is no longer an option.
It has become a business
imperative.

You can sense the character of these companies in the second half of their life cycle when you deal with them as a customer. The top people in the organization are in "staff" and "management" jobs.

Those positions with direct customer contact are now held by the lowest-paid people in the business — mostly clerks.

These days many companies have gone the extra mile in the name of efficiencies leaving you to deal with "hot lines" and endless muzak in place of clerical staff. Can you recall what life as a customer was like at the start of the business cycle? The people who dealt with the customer were the best and smartest people in the business. They may even have been the founders of the business. Remember?

We should never forget that this plummet into the internal efficiency vertigo only happens to successful businesses. The failures disappear off the radar screen before they have the chance to become obsessed with efficiency and lose sight of the customer.

For successful companies, this constant drift from innovation to evolution requires a quantum shift in corporate thinking, from evolution to revolution. The state of the corporation at this stage is analogous to an ark ready to tackle a tidal wave.

An ark may have been the absolutely right organizational model for the last 50 years, but with an economic tidal wave on the way, surfboards (small, nimble young companies) may be more appropriate. But typically, you are caught in the culture trap. You can't recreate the entrepreneurial culture of the first half of the business life cycle amidst the "efficiency" culture of the second half of the business life cycle.

If you do nothing (ie remain addicted to the ark model) you will be wiped out by the disruptive forces of the New Economy.

Radical innovation is no longer an option. It is a business imperative.

Product performance

Sustaining innovation – EVOLUTIONARY!

Performance demanded at high end of market

Performance demanded at low end of market

New innovators!

Radical innovation – REVOLUTIONARY!

Today

Time

Given these economic and commercial opportunities, why do so many great companies fail in the face of disruptive technologies?

To understand the above, let's look at the work of Clayton Christensen, which provides the most powerful evidence of the challenges faced in this regard by large successful companies. I have found it useful with our clients to map his thinking onto the concept of business and product life cycles.

When new companies design their products, the products in their initial manifestations almost never meet up to the performance levels demanded at the low end of the market. It is only when their products break through this barrier that they begin to be taken seriously by "the establishment".

Clayton notes that it is not only at the bottom end of the market that these barriers exist.

Similarly, at the high end of the market, there are performance levels beyond which the customer no longer attaches value to additional enhancements or functionality.

In our everyday lives we encounter such products all too often. How much of the functionality of the cellphone do you personally use? How many more features on a video recorder would you willingly pay for?

Let's take the example of Microsoft Excel, a product already rated as "too functional" by most of its users. Chances are that you are one of hundreds of millions of Excel users. You most likely use less than 10 per cent of Excel's functionality. Wouldn't it be nice if you could pay for only the 10 per cent you use? Will you really value the improved functionality of the next release? How much more will you be prepared to pay?

Often, **radical** innovation
is **not**
a rational **financial** decision

Yet, despite all indications from the market, Excel is being constantly enhanced by a large team at Microsoft. The market clearly does not require more functionality. What it really requires is a simpler and more flexibly priced product.

Will it come from Microsoft? Little chance. And that is the innovator's dilemma. What is an obvious opportunity to the new innovators is often considered economic suicide for the existing market leader.

How can the executives of the Excel development team break trust by shedding the dream of producing the world's best spreadsheet program? After all these years of constant celebration, how can they now decide that innovation is no longer such a noble goal?

Often, radical innovation is not a rational financial decision.

The new products are often simpler, cheaper and more convenient. As if that wasn't enough...the margins are lower.

Also, the typical new customers are considered "insignificant". The early adopters often represent the least profitable customers – young people, students. And guess what? The current "blue chip" customers don't want to use the new products. Probably because they don't know how to, and aren't willing to learn.

Just think of the early attitudes of the big corporates to the personal computer.

How can such a small computer with such a "Mickey Mouse" operating system be a real threat to the mainframe?

The PC couldn't really be taken seriously.

And, look at those naïve new innovators...the products are less reliable and they don't even make any profit.

So large successful companies don't do it.

They don't innovate radically, even as life in the business world outside evolves and gets ever more hostile for the old life forms.

Even more surprising is that Clayton Christensen's research has shown that sound decisions by good managers consistently lead to failure. Just by planning better, working harder and focusing on the customer, things start coming off the rails.

Improving product features and efficiencies is useless if the products are losing their relevance in the eyes of the customer. Good management is simply not enough in the face of disruptive technologies.

We should also never forget the inherent difference between sustaining technologies and disruptive technologies: sustaining technologies tend to improve product performance, while disruptive technologies often result in worse product performance, at least initially.

The big cycles – Kondratieff

Nikolai Dmitrijewitsch Kondratieff (1892–1938), published his essay "Long Economic Cycles" in 1922. This study of the long cycles in capitalist economies did not find favour with his superiors, and Kondratieff ended his life in Siberian exile, never quite having found answers to the two big questions: "Why?" and "So what?"

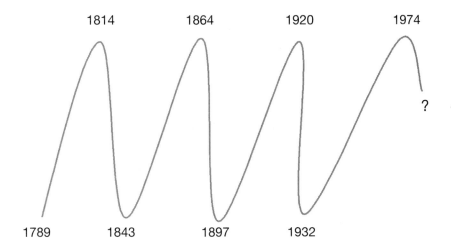

The big cycles – Schumpeter

Yosef Schumpeter, Harvard professor and one-time Austrian Minister of Finance, believed the driving force behind the Kondratieff waves was innovation, by which he meant not only new inventions, but any "change in the method of supplying commodities".

In his book *Business Cycles*, published in 1939, Schumpeter associated each of Kondratieff's long waves with specific innovations in technology and commerce. *The Economist* of February 1999 included a now-famous survey on innovation called "Industry gets religion" from which this chart was taken.

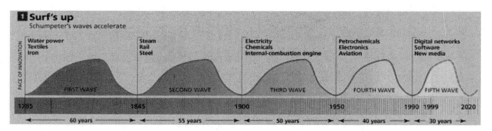

Schumpeter envisioned an economy whose growth was propelled by the entrepreneurial spirit. He believed that continuous entrepreneurship was necessary to drive growth. He coined the term "creative destruction" to describe the disruptive effect of true innovation.

It is only now, in the first years of the 21st Century, that we are again reminded of the destructive aspects of innovation in our day-to-day business life.

Innovation is not the result of one or two innovators innovating once or twice. Innovation at an economic level is the result of hundreds of thousands of entrepreneurs innovating continuously over a long period of time. This is what creates powerful economic waves.

Destruction!	Today	Yesterday	
Railroad employees	231,000	2,076,000	1920
Carriage, harness makers	*	109,000	1900
Telegraph operators	8,000	75,000	1920
Boilermakers	*	74,000	1920
Cobblers	25,000	102,000	1900
Blacksmiths	*	238,000	1910
Watchmakers	*	101,000	1920
Switchboard operators	213,000	421,000	1970
Farm workers	851,000	11,500,000	1910
Total	1,328,000	14,396,000	

Creation!	Today	Yesterday	
Pilots, mechanics	232,000	0	1900
Medical technicians	1,380,000	0	1900
Engineers	1,850,000	38,000	1900
Computer programmers	1,290,000	*	1960
Fax machine workers	699,000	0	1980
Car mechanics	864,000	0	1900
Truck, bus and taxi drivers	3,330,000	0	1900
Professional athletes	77,000	0	1920
TV and radio announcers	30,000	*	1930
Electricians, electronic engineers	711,000	51,000	1900
Optometrists	62,000	*	1910
Total	10,525,000	<100,000	

Every massive wave of innovation brings with it economic activity and sometimes spectacular growth. The bigger the success and the steeper the growth, the greater the risk of simultaneous destruction – of old competitors, of old ways of doing business and of old ways of work.

The negative effect of innovation often manifests most publicly as a loss of jobs. Opposite are some examples from data provided by the US Bureau of Census. (An * in a cell indicates figures of less than 5000 jobs.)

Great and sustained innovation always brings with it a fair share of destruction – of jobs, whole industries and competitors, cherished old ways of doing things, consumer traditions, etc.

Any business leader who seriously wants to lead a truly innovative company has to be ready to manage the creative side of innovation, as well as the rather more difficult destructive consequences of innovation.

This dark side of innovation is exactly the reason why executives shy away from real radical innovation. Let's explore why the winds of creative destruction can inhibit innovation, and what you can do about it.

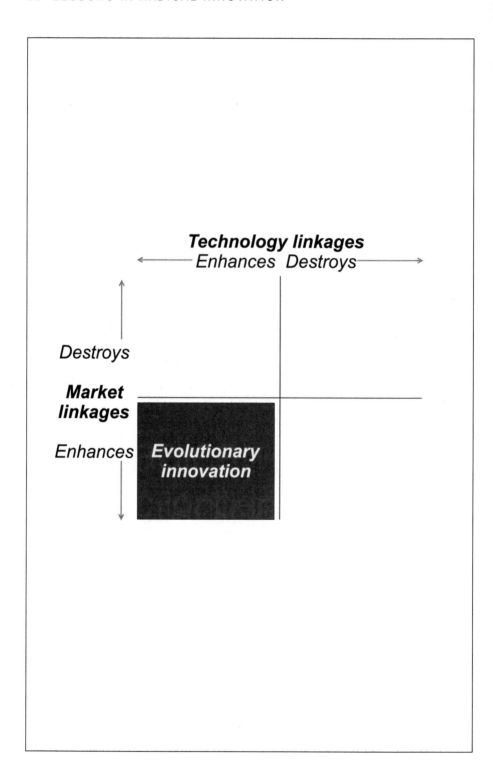

The winds of creative destruction

In 1985, Abernathy and Clark published a groundbreaking research paper in the publication *Research Policy*. I found their table to be of great relevance in the context of innovation today. Within FutureWorld we use these concepts with our clients, and have developed the original model to meet their current needs.

The basic matrix consists of two axes that indicate the relative levels of creative destruction in two dimensions:

- **Technology linkages**: The new innovation either enhances existing technology usage, skills, platforms, investments, etc, or destroys them.

- **Market linkages**: The new innovation either enhances existing market linkages, channels, business partners and processes, or threatens to destroy them.

Any innovation that both enhances current market relationships and the current technology base would be characterized as evolutionary innovation in this model. Let's use an example to clarify the matrix.

The scene is an Innovation Board meeting at the head office of a large airline.

Stakeholders and staff from across the group are represented. On the table is an innovative proposal to enhance the airline's reservation system, which boasts more than a decade of investment and the support of thousands of technical staffers. Now, according to the proposal, the system will be upgraded to give travel agents access to really innovative new services, featuring faster speed and simpler interfaces.

Based on this proposal, the current reservation system would be enhanced (not destroyed) and the market linkages (the travel agents) would enjoy significant benefits and ease of use. In a survey, the travel agents perceived the proposal as "really innovative". Existing technical staff would be able to handle all additions to the systems using their existing expertise.

This is a very low-risk approach, creating incremental benefits and a sure thing. This is what we call evolutionary innovation.

Technology linkages

←——— Enhances Destroys ————→

Destroys

Market linkages

Enhances

| **Evolutionary innovation** | **Disruptive innovation** (Disrupting the technology base) |

The moment the airline steps out of the bottom-left box the potential destruction begins. Let's say the airline now decides to go a step further.

A task-force recommends that

the **"old" reservation system has come to the end** of its useful life and that a radical new approach is needed.

It decides to invest in a new Internet-based reservation system, using all the latest technologies that promise to give orders of magnitude improvement in terms of access by the travel agents ("Anywhere – anytime" is to be the slogan) with the added benefit of significantly lower costs. So, this approach will significantly enhance their current market linkages.

The problem is that their current technical skills are not adequate to do this and re-training is not an option.

The average age of their current technical staff is between 40 and 50. Problem is, the skills they need for the new systems are typically found in 18- to 30-year-olds.

The airline decides to outsource the new development and to have a phased lay-off of the current experts in the technology of their "old" reservation system. More than 500 existing jobs are threatened by this new innovation as the old technology linkages are destroyed. Union action is anticipated.

When the executive team meets to assess the risk of this new project, the internal turmoil created by this "radical" step is considered by many to be too risky for the reward of a more effective network of travel agents. The team decides on a more evolutionary approach based on enhancements of the current reservation systems. Get the picture? Conflict, and significant innovation, avoided. It has taken the safe evolutionary option.

This approach is sometimes called "faking innovation". The inherent assumption here is that the punishment for failure is larger than the reward for success.

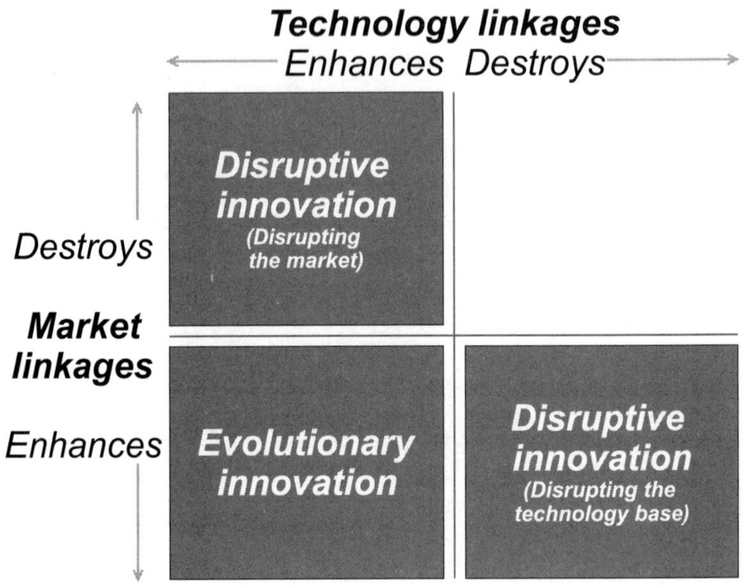

Technology linkages

←——— Enhances Destroys ———→

Destroys

Market linkages

Enhances

Disruptive innovation
(Disrupting the market)

Evolutionary innovation

Disruptive innovation
(Disrupting the technology base)

Now imagine the scenario if the airline decides to build a very user-friendly front-end to the system, and make that directly available to customers via its website. This would allow all customers with Internet access to bypass the travel agents and make their own reservations. Say the airline decides to sweeten the pill for the customers by offering them a 10 per cent discount for booking and paying online. While this approach would not be disruptive to the airline's technology linkages (it would in fact build on their investments) it would potentially create an extremely negative response from the travel agents. This too would be an example of disruptive innovation – this time disrupting the market linkages.

British Airways in fact considered this disruptive option, even going so far as to create a separate airline, *Go!*, to offer this innovation without offending their travel agents. *Go!* was similar to BA – essentially it was the *"Budget BA"* – but you had to book via telephone or the Internet. No tickets were issued and savings were passed on to the passenger.

Think about the lengths executives will go, to avoid destroying the current market linkages! While many airlines offer online reservations and purchasing of tickets, few have had the courage to price these lower – even if the savings are substantial – for fear of offending their tried and trusted channel. *Go!* was subsequently disposed of by British Airways in July 2001 for £110 million, way beyond the initial investment of £25 million.

Now, let's go back to our fictitious airline's Innovation Board meeting.

Suddenly a young executive at the back of the room stands up and asks: "If we are going to be radical, and potentially alienate the travel agent community by threatening part of its customer base that has access to the Internet, why don't we get really radical and take away its total customer base?

"The problem with the Internet is that it doesn't cover the entire market for travel reservations, we need an infrastructure that every customer has access to. Why don't we create a joint venture with the mobile phone companies and put a new reservation facility into every mobile phone. Imagine this – just hold down the # key for five seconds and you have direct access to our reservation system. To all intents and purposes, every one of our customers has a mobile phone and all we need is some really sexy software. We can share the savings with any customer who books this way and pass, say, a 10 per cent saving directly on to the customer."

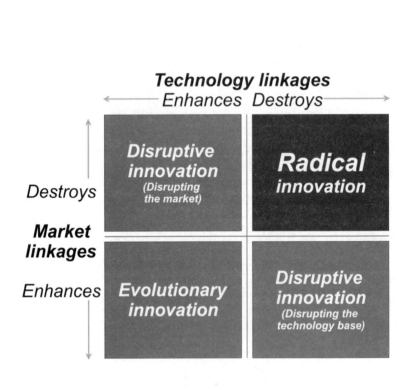

The HR executive ponders this for a moment and then concludes: "But we don't have any of these skills available in-house! Also, with our current profile in the market as an employer I don't believe we can attract the right kind of skills into this organization – we'd have to source these skills through some sort of partnership. Even the mobile phone companies have very few of these skills. I can just imagine the enthusiasm we'd get from the folks in IT – once this new system is bedded down they would see the writing on the wall for their own jobs. I don't believe they would be able or willing to be re-skilled."

The young executive is unbowed: "The travel agents will hate us but the customer will see real savings immediately. This innovation could make us the darling of business and leisure travellers the world over. Imagine the ad campaign – '*We're as far away as your # key!*' The unions may hate us but we'll put this airline onto the high road – we'll be leading the airline industry into the future. Can we afford not to do this?"

Now that's what I call radical innovation.

Innovation that simultaneously destroys the technology base – by leap-frogging into unproven disruptive technology – plus the market linkages, by making it very difficult for travel agents to compete with the airline. They couldn't do it on price so they would have to develop really innovative new value-adding services to keep their customers.

This creative–destruction matrix has become a powerful tool in the work we do with our clients. We use it to create an innovation profile for a business, together with their executive team, in less than an hour. This is how it works.

- Identify the top activities (perhaps ten or so) in which you currently focus resources in your business.

- Represent each one by a bubble that represents your view of the size of the revenue or investment and put these bubbles where you believe they fit in the matrix, depending on the degree to which they potentially enhance or destroy the current market linkages and technology.

- Step back and consider the overall profile of your business – what kind of business are you in terms of innovation?

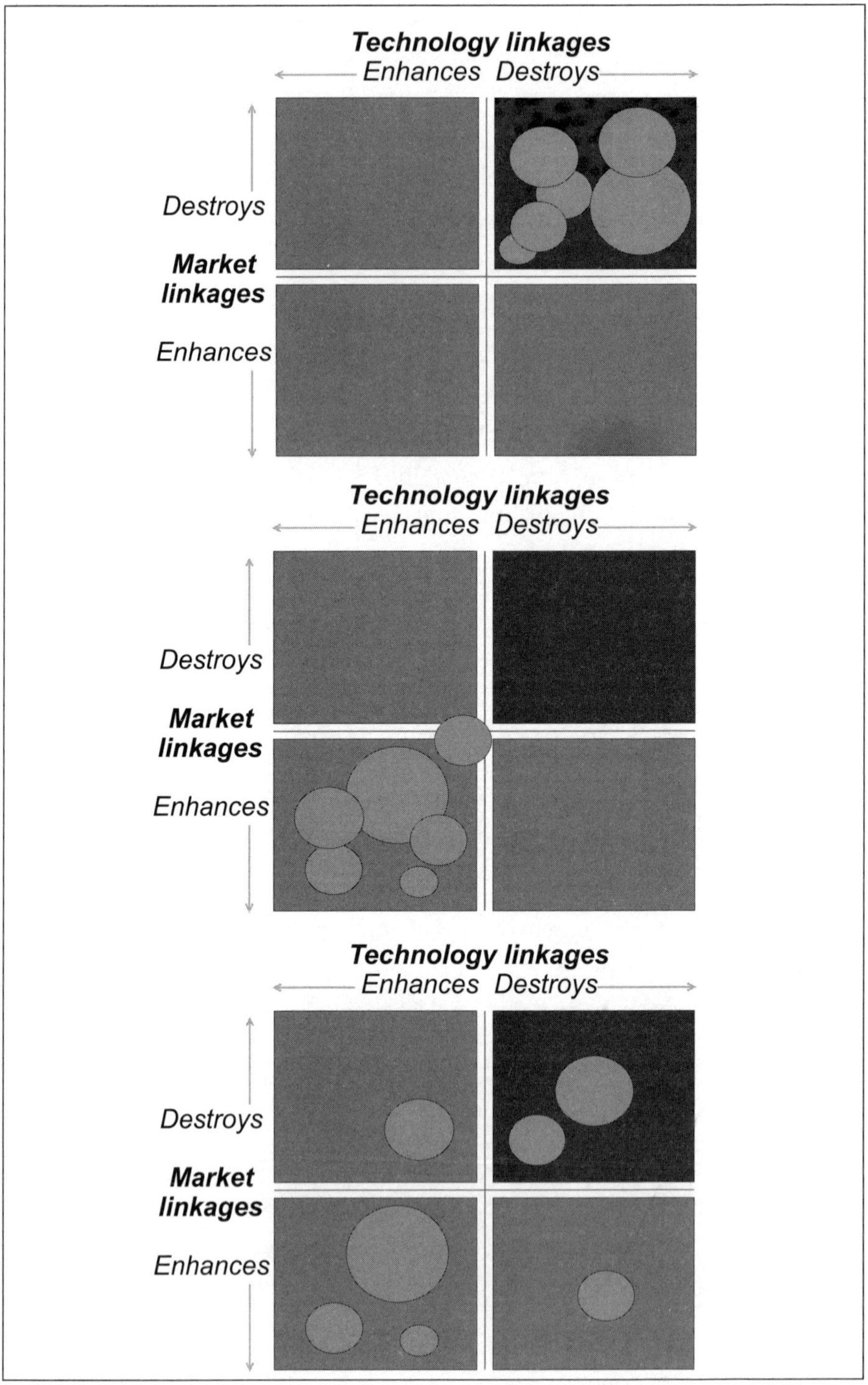

Technology linkages
Enhances Destroys

Destroys

Market linkages

Enhances

Technology linkages
Enhances Destroys

Destroys

Market linkages

Enhances

Technology linkages
Enhances Destroys

Destroys

Market linkages

Enhances

The possibilities are of course endless, but let's say you created a matrix that looked something like the first diagram opposite.

What kind of a company would you be dealing with?

Most likely a very new company. Great ideas, great people, great innovators, but not yet a proven approach to market. They may not yet be generating much revenue. Certainly, you would not yet be generating any profit. Perhaps the profile of a typical young dot com business, regarded by analysts as very exciting but very risky. Based on the experience of the past decade only 5–10 per cent of these companies ever make it to profitability.

Look at the next matrix opposite. What kind of a business would this be?

Most likely this is a real cash-cow business. An established, well-managed business that's simply not running any high-risk projects. It is not investing in its future success. It probably dedicates no more than 1–2 per cent of its revenues to innovation. It is highly regarded by investment analysts for delivering consistent returns over a long period of time.

But most likely the business has no future. In fast-changing markets you have to innovate faster than others in the marketplace. The above is a classical example of a company that is selling its future to pay for short-term financial returns.

We realize that an ideal business is most likely one that looks something like the bottom matrix opposite. A well-balanced business that has a great "current reality", has clearly decided on its "desired future", and is investing in it.

It most likely allocates around 10–20 per cent of its revenues to radical projects.

The reality is that only radical innovation builds future markets and ensures future relevance.

Only **radical** innovation **builds** future markets and ensures **future relevance.**

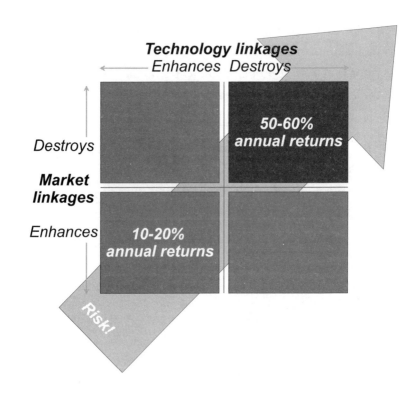

In summary, here are a few things about the matrix we should never forget.

1. Risk increases exponentially from bottom-left to top-right

Choose your own number for accepted failure rates in the radical innovation box. Companies we have seen have had practical experiences in failure rates of anything from 50–90 per cent. The only rule that comes through constantly is: if you're going to fail, fail very quickly. There is nothing more painful to the bottom line or morale than slow failure.

2. Potential returns from successful radical innovations far outweigh those from evolutionary innovations

One company we worked with used this long-term rule of thumb based on its own practical experience: 10–20 per cent returns annually from evolutionary innovation, 50–60 per cent returns annually from radical innovation.

3. It does not take any more effort or energy to be radical than to be evolutionary

Either way you're going to be busy all the time. It may just take a little more passion, confidence and leadership.

4. Don't ever put people in the wrong box

If you want to be a conservative company that is seen as an evolutionary innovator (there may be nothing wrong with that), then don't hire radical innovators. At best, they will be totally frustrated and will not stay long. At worst they will take down a part of your business with them. Similarly, if you have bred incrementalists, don't suddenly ask them to be radical – you will scare them to death and they will think the company has gone mad.

Technology linkages
Enhances Destroys

Destroys

**Market
linkages**

Enhances

5. Radical innovation is time-bound, today's "radical" is tomorrow's "norm"

Imagine the matrix as if there is a river flowing from top-right to bottom-left.

The bigger and more visible the innovation,

the faster it will be swept towards "the norm".

Any radical idea (in the top-right box) will, over time, be swept to the bottom-left, it will become absolutely the norm. Our "river of time" spares no large objects. The largest most-recognized innovations are often the first to be commoditized. Any new innovations to this "old" idea will then be considered evolutionary. Radical innovation is a constant drive to fill the top-right box with radical new projects.

You must threaten your own business before someone else does.

Sometimes too, radical innovation seems to turn back on itself. What seemed like a great idea for a long period of time, suddenly loses its relevance when the context changes. You're never safe. It's not only if you're heading up Intel that you need to be paranoid!

Every innovation, no matter how radical, is dramatically shaped by the rivers of time that run through all of our markets.

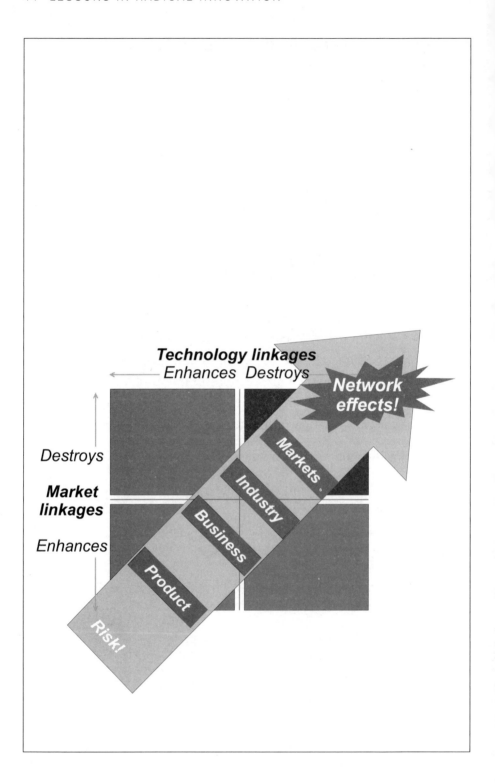

The source and consequence of innovation

From the innovator's viewpoint innovation can arise almost anywhere and from any source. Most typically it is at component or product level where the primary innovations occur. But it is only when these cascade up the food chain that their real value is felt.

Radical innovation at component level is perhaps the most impressive. Consider how a simple idea like tilting the read/write head in a VCR turned it from a niche market in recording studios into the second most popular consumer appliance in history.

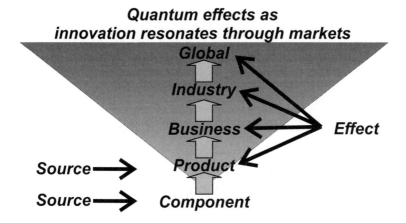

Evolutionary innovation is relatively risk-free and companies that innovate at this level generally focus on improvements at the "product" level (see opposite) – making them faster, better, cheaper.

Going up the innovation/risk ladder in our matrix you enter the domain of innovation at the total business level, but of course risk increases exponentially.

Beyond this the company enters the domain of radical innovation (in the top-right box of the matrix). Here it is typical to encounter high-risk innovation that will change an entire industry – think back to American Airlines original airline reservation strategy. Ultimately, radical innovations have the power to change global markets.

Brand Pretorius, CEO of McCarthy Retail, puts it succinctly: "Today competition is no longer between products, its between business models. And you can't get there through evolutionary change."

Reaching the pinnacle of innovation is not about more effort or more capital investment. It's about quality of thinking (thought leadership) and about bold follow-through for new projects (breakthrough implementation).

The companies that achieve these levels of innovation are typically held up to be role models way beyond their specific industry.

At the pinnacle of radical innovation lie those "network effects", where a particular innovation is so profound that it allows the innovator to draw economic value almost anytime anyone in the industry moves. Consider the way Qualcomm has built such a powerful position for itself in the global mobile phone market. Almost every time anyone anywhere manufactures a cell phone, Qualcomm receives "A Few Dollars More" in royalties. The more successful the industry becomes overall, the better off it is. This is a utopian annuity income. No wonder it has been one of the most successful stocks on Nasdaq over the past decade.

This is the law of increasing returns in action.

Consider a bank that publishes all of its competitors' mortgage rates on its website. Wouldn't it become the first choice portal for such information? Could it not attract more consumers than competitors who only published their own rates? Can you imagine how hard you would work to make sure that your rates were constantly competitive if you knew that you had to expose your own rates to the best in the market, on your website every day.

It doesn't make sense until you begin to think disruptively! The network effect is the pinnacle we strive for each time we work with a client on radical innovation.

We ask: Where are the network effects?

The answer is seldom obvious. It is a relentless pursuit beyond the "One Right Answer".

Whenever we reach what we think is the end – you know the feeling... "That's it. Finally we have the answer" – we say, "That's not good enough. Let's try to be a bit more radical. Let's go beyond. How can we capitalize on more network effects?"

Reaching the pinnacle of innovation is not about more effort or more capital investment. It is about quality of thinking (thought leadership) and about bold follow-through for the new projects that emerge (breakthrough implementation).

Today, **competition**
is no longer between products,
its between business models –
and you can't get there
through **evolutionary**
change.

Because of its fractal nature, radical innovation

is highly **uncertain,**

unpredictable

– you must learn to keep the faith.

This is not just about being risk-averse. It's also about strategic patience. Radical projects are sporadic, with many stops and starts, many blind alleys – it's not unlike the fearful ancient medina of Fez.

There is constant death and rebirth – relevance changes with the market, needs are never the same the second time around – you need to keep your mind actively open. Remember it's like a parachute, it tends to work best when open.

New ideas never stop coming. Problems never disappear. Reality is always messy. Never shut your mind to emerging late news. Better to hear it now than when it's too late. The cost of changing later in the innovation project will always be higher than it is today. Once you reach the pinnacle and capitalize on network effects you will realize that the payback is biological – effects are volatile, unpredictable and non-linear. There are sudden bifurcation points that can go up or down. Butterfly effects are everywhere – very small changes can have massive consequences.

At times, everything appears to be counter-intuitive – management practices that work for incremental innovation often deter radical innovation.

There seems to be little evidence of success in implementing deliberate and systematic approaches to radical innovation, but there are many practical examples of useful lessons that we can explore. If you accept that innovation is both a "machine" and a "garden" then you will see that we have to explore both worlds – the mechanistic and intuitive.

Radical innovation
is primarily driven through
the "unreasonable" behaviour
of individuals.
Without personal passion,
the cows of innovation don't calve!

At the heart of these lessons in radical innovation are bold visionary individuals. Despite the fact that most established corporations have spent decades trying to identify innovation processes that can be driven by the organization centrally, the truth behind radical innovation is the exact opposite – radical innovation is primarily driven through the "unreasonable" behaviour of individuals. Without personal passion, the cows of innovation don't calve!

But how can the corporation possibly manage such a disorderly process? The people we need, these entrepreneurs, seem to be totally "impatient and unreasonable" and unlikely to want to be a part of our current corporate culture.

Managing entrepreneurs seems to be an oxymoron. So how do you do it?

What we'll learn as we share the experiences of innovators is that you have to learn to herd cats!

That's what the rest of this book is all about: passionate individuals, entrepreneurial behaviour, turning the latest tools into viable technologies, and whole dollops of strategic impatience!

We'll meet innovators who are leading the world in their thinking, and leading global markets through their products and services. Let's see what they did. Let's see how they succeeded, and why they failed.

In the final chapters, I'll be back to pull together some threads that run through each of the stories and introduce you to a process we've developed to help create a context for radical innovation by our clients. We call this process Strategic Thinking and Strategic Action™. Perhaps you'll find it useful in your business too.

Get ready for an exhilarating and passionate ride.

Changing the game

Don't just change the rules – change what you are

How a venerable French **water and waste-management** company **transformed** itself into a multimedia communications conglomerate

It begins with a single drop of rain, falling from a stormy sky. Then a multitude of droplets, merging, converging, flowing into puddles, streams and rivers, surging towards the common destiny of a whole that is greater than the sum of its parts.

The all-enveloping ocean, source of life on this planet, pooled from millions of individual channels, individual tributaries, individual torrents of unstoppable energy.

Water.

Break it down to its constituent molecules – one part hydrogen, two parts oxygen – and you have the solid basis of a liquid asset that can quench a thirst, nurture a plantation, and build a business empire.

Consider the case of the Compagnie Générale des Eaux, founded in Paris in 1853 by the Emperor Napoleon III, who is better remembered by the history books for leading France to a crushing defeat against the Prussian Army of Prince Otto von Bismarck.

Campagnie Générale des Eaux – the source of Vivendi Universal

As an industrialist, Napoleon proved to be a man of greater vision, his ultimate victory being the wellspring of a company that today pumps more than 3000 billion litres of water a year into the homes of more than 70 million consumers across Europe. And yet, man cannot live on *eaux* alone.

In the space of one-and-a-half centuries, the tributaries and subsidiaries of the Compagnie Générale des Eaux grew to encompass everything from waste management to construction to transport to property to communications. Many streams, many rivers, one ocean.

But by 1995, the company is drowning in debt – $9.6 billion – and wallowing under the weight of its own conglomerate bureaucracy. It is time for a change. A distillation. A diversion of energies into other streams, other channels.

Water is the source of this company; who says water has to be its future?

And so, from within Générale des Eaux's vast network of interests and operations, an element of the purest oxygen – a controlling stake of a multilingual pay television channel called Canal Plus, broadcasting to ten countries in Europe – is isolated, invigorated and exposed to the light of new possibility.

Buoyed by waves of radical change, in a world of ever-shifting boundaries, the future of Générale des Eaux is, quite literally, up in the air.

The pay station, with its popular bouquet of sport, travel, lifestyle and movies, serves as the springboard for an intricate series of mergers and acquisitions, mutations and transformations. Result? A venerable French utility company, born in the 19th Century, becomes a global media giant in the 21st.

Vivendi Universal is born.

Here, the primary asset is a thing called "information", broken down to its core constituents of education, entertainment, communication.

Here, the delinquent rap of Eminem, the metallic pop of Bon Jovi, the Brontosaurian megastars of *Jurassic Park III*, titillate and assault the senses as they surge in criss-crossing streams towards a whole that is, once again, greater than the sum of its parts. Music, movies, television, books, newspapers, websites, software, cellular communication networks.

Here is an empire built on bits and bytes of data, on digital signals and impulses, on words and pictures and sound. And here is the Emperor: a man whose lively eyes, wry smile and Gallic charm belie a driving ambition that extends across the Channel, across the Atlantic, across the world.

In France they call him *j6m*, a friendly abbreviation for the six m's by which he earns his nickname: Jean-Marie Messier, *moi-meme, maître du monde*. Jean-Marie Messier, Master of the Universe. Far from being perturbed by the nickname, he embraces it as part of his own public branding: "Some people might see me as a megalomaniac," he admits, "but to me, it is just a reminder not to take myself too seriously."

In part, the grandly-mocking appellation, eagerly adopted by *j6m* as the title of his business autobiography, is a tribute to the business deal that put Monsieur Messier on the map.

Hands across the waters...Vivendi announces merger with
Seagram and Canalt on 20 June 2000

When Vivendi acquired Seagram for $23 billion in June 2000, it was more than a simple marriage between a European company founded on H_2O and a Canadian conglomerate best known for its spirits and wines.

Winning the box office battle... a scene from Gladiator

The real mix was a scintillating cocktail of media interests that included Hollywood's legendary Universal Studios (responsible for such mega-hits as *Gladiator* and *American Pie 2*) and the world's largest music company, Universal Music (everyone from U2 to Bjork to Shania Twain).

A mere six months after making the first overtures to Seagram, Messier had built himself a multimedia empire that could compete on equal turf, if not equal terms, with such global giants as AOL Time Warner, Viacom and the Walt Disney Company.

Son of France, Citizen of the World, Messier shifts his base from the heart of Paris to midtown Manhattan, where his office in the Seagram Building, one of the city's most elegant skyscrapers, gives him a commanding view of the universe beneath his feet.

Vivendi lists on the New York Stock Exchange

Reflecting on a position that grants him power in the boardroom, influence over the lives of millions, and the aura of glamour that is inevitably associated with life in the fast lane of the multimedia entertainment business, Messier makes no attempt to disguise his boyish enthusiasm.

"I feel great,"

he announces.

"I wouldn't want it any other way.

I am the happiest man on earth."

And yet, there are those – analysts, commentators, rivals – who say Messier commands his position not through dazzling entrepreneurial flair or boldness of vision, but through sheer force of charisma and an instinctive ability to strike a deal.

There are those who point out that Vivendi remains, in essence, an old-economy conglomerate, with only a quarter of its operating profit coming in from the high-tech and multimedia companies that define the new economy.

But the fact remains: Jean-Marie Messier is the man who transformed a company, and in so doing, transformed the very landscape in which it operates.

"As one advances," he reflects, "one disturbs. Some people don't like that, so they brand you an agitator."

But if Messier does have revolutionary tendencies, he must belong to the faction that believes in changing the system from within. It's worth noting that between the Emperor Napoleon (1853) and the Master of the Universe, Jean-Marie Messier (1996), only nine Frenchmen have served as Chairman of the Compagnie Générale des Eaux.

That's evidence enough of an organization where stability, continuity and discretion have ploughed the tried-and-trusted path to progress. An organization that has always taken pride in its overwhelming dominance of the territories it knows best: top energy company in Europe, leading household and industrial waste-management company in Europe, Number One private transport operator in Europe.

And yet, as the end of the millennium approached, this was a company in a rut. A company with too many divisions and subsidiaries, too many managers, too much baggage. In 1994, enter Jean-Marie Messier, a mere 37 years of age, fresh from a stint at Lazard Frères investment bank, where he was the youngest partner in the firm's history, and before that, the French Civil Service, where he was the youngest-ever Chief of Staff of the Finance Ministry.

But this was no ordinary investment banker, no ordinary civil servant. This was a young man with a mission. With perfect charm, with ruthless efficiency, he gets down to business. Out go the surplus staff, as Europe's largest private employer trims its 245,000-strong workforce by 10 per cent.

Out go layers and levels of hierarchy, as Messier cuts his inner circle of managers from more than 80 to less than ten. Out go some $25 billion worth of poorly-performing holdings, from property to healthcare to investment.

What's left? A lean, mean communications business, floating atop of a solid core of water services and waste management.

But it wasn't pay television, and it wasn't cellular telephony, that stirred the new Chairman's imagination as he steered the company towards the 21st Century. What excited him was the potential of a medium that could quench man's thirst for knowledge, open the floodgates of information, and flow freely across the boundaries of culture and nationhood.

A medium as ubiquitous,

as pervasive, as H_2O itself.

The Internet.

"I don't think there is a more formidable tool with which to revolutionize our way of life," says Messier. "The Internet provides access to knowledge and information, but more than that, it provides power to individuals.

"Thanks to the Internet, the individual can speak and make himself heard across the borders of space and time. The consequences of this are immense. In a matter of seconds, you can communicate any idea you want, to anyone, anywhere in the world. The Internet is the libertarian network par excellence."

At the same time, of course, Messier is a businessman, and he knows that the Internet is more than an instrument of liberty, equality, fraternity. It is an instrument, even more revolutionary, of profit beyond imagining. But first, you have to get the formula right.

For just as hydrogen and oxygen bonded to form the basis of Générale des Eaux's original business, so would two key elements have to be fused to build its future. Content and delivery.

In January 2000, the template for what will become the business model of the 21st Century is struck with the daring merger of AOL, America's biggest Internet service-provider, and Time Warner, the motion-picture and publishing conglomerate.

Suddenly, there is **one giant company** with the power to produce media – movies, magazines, TV, books, music – and the power to distribute it into the homes of millions of consumers, through its own vast network of channels and platforms.

One of Seagram's breakthrough brands...Captain Morgan rum

In France, Jean-Marie Messier is galvanized into action. He takes control of the French division of AOL, left behind by the American merger, to add the missing ingredient of online infrastructure to his rapidly-brewing mix of communications combustibles: satellite television, cellular telephony, software, publishing.

It is only the beginning. In order to turn his company into a big global player, he needs to find a big global partner. And that's where Seagram comes in.

Much like the Compagnie Générale des Eaux, Seagram is a venerable business empire in the process of re-inventing itself, from producer, marketer and distributor of spirits and wines (Chivas Regal, Captain Morgan, Martell, Stirling Vineyards) to publisher, distributor and manufacturer of movies, music, television.

"Seagram had the content," says Messier. "Vivendi had the mechanisms for delivery. Here we had the perfect marriage of minds, media and markets. But still, it was only the beginning."

For Jean-Marie Messier, Vivendi Universal is something more than the latest incarnation of a company that has somehow always been in the business of pumping a life-sustaining force through an ever-expanding network of pipes, channels and conduits.

It is something more than the "multi-cultural, multimedia company" that has brought Messier's bold trans-Atlantic vision to life.

Vivendi Universal is about the business of building bridges; about the art of turning puddles into streams, streams into rivers, rivers into oceans. Think of a world where your cellular telephone and your computer and your television and your satellite decoder and your MP3-player and your PDA are all part of a single, seamless network for sharing information and knowledge.

Think of a world where every medium of communication – the printed page, the Internet, the cathode-ray tube, the silver screen, the digital handset – feeds on and feeds off every other medium in its orbit.

Think of a world without barriers and boundaries, a world where the shape of your past does not have to dictate the shape of your future. Think of a world where you, too, by directing and diverting the flow of your energies and ambitions, can be *moi-meme, maître du monde*: Master of the Universe.

All it takes is a simple fusion
of elements that are **already in abundance.**

All it takes,
when you get right down to it…

…is a single drop of rain.

MY LESSONS LEARNT ?

Lessons learnt

Your business future is not tethered to the past

If you have "a group", run it as a group, or break it up

The future comprises many streams, many channels, but it's all one interconnected ocean

Information does not necessarily need to be free

It's not about the technology, it's about the power it gives to individuals who embrace it

Charm, coupled with efficiency, can move old economy mountains

Every opportunity is perishable

The entrepreneur is not someone with unique access to resources. An entrepreneur is someone who fuses elements that are available to all, in abundance, and creates massive new customer value

By all means be Master of the Universe – but don't take yourself too seriously! If you feel great, say so! If you're happy, share it

How business life cycles destroy innovation...

On 2 July 2002 Jean-Marie Messier wept as he left the Vivendi HO in Paris. He had been pushed to resign as CEO. The press speculated that the company had run out of patience just before they ran out of money, perhaps not unkindly.

No longer was there room for the **"renegade innovator"**, "the **flamboyant** CEO" or "brash, abrasive and confident".

On 7 November 2002 the new CEO Jean-René Fourtou announced that Vivendi would sell their remaining stake in Vivendi Environmental, shedding their link to the national water business that spawned the now sprawling global media empire. The financial boost would enable Vivendi to fight off the unwanted approaches of joint venture partner Vodafone to purchase Vivendi's share of French mobile phone operator Cegetel.

Fourtou's actions were variously described as "institutional wisdom", "authority born of experience", a "diplomatic power house" who promised to deliver "consistent results" – classic characteristics of a CEO and a company in the second half of its life cycle.

For more about these life cycles see chapter one.

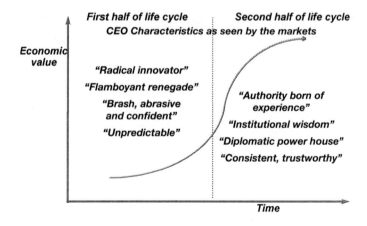

...and the successful CEOs who spawned it!

There was no longer room for the 'business rock star', the darling of the press when everything was booming. The messy public blood-letting that followed finally brought the Vivendi hero of just a few years previous to his knees.

The Romans had a saying for it;

"Those whom the gods want to destroy they first make famous".

Every successful CEO who has developed a reputation for radical innovation must learn these lessons.

There is no room for the radical innovator, her skills or attitudes in the second half of the corporate life cycle. The moment the shareholders and market predictability become more important than that which made you successful, that is the moment to make your exit.

Take it on the chin, make your exit! It's not that suddenly your skills are no longer appreciated – the market simply no longer sees them as relevant to the second half of the business life cycle.

Do it gracefully. Do it before you have to. Do it while you can still afford to. Don't wait too long, like Jobs and Messier, don't be drugged by the personal glory the press heaps on you. Leave before you get to the pinnacle.

It's better to leave two years too early, than one minute too late.

Now, read the book and share a myriad of other lessons that will get to this unenviable point of choice!

3

Eating yourself

A blueprint for cannibalizing your own business

How two of England's most venerable institutions, Prudential and the Co-op, threw tradition to the winds and allowed their banking divisions to be swallowed by upstarts of their own creation... branchless online banks called Egg and smile

Like almost any man of the post World War II economic boom, he wore a hat to work, carried an attaché case, and dressed for success in a suit of synthetic fibre. He would arrive on your doorstep, extend a cordial greeting, and ask if he might borrow a few precious moments of your time.

Then, in the comfort of your lounge, he would remove his hat, open his case, and set out to sell you the secrets of a better tomorrow. He was your friend, your adviser, your guide through troubled waters.

He was the

"Man from the Pru".

Door-to-door ambassador for the largest life assurance company in the UK, he was the face and the fortune of a range of products that were "never bought, always sold". Insurance, assurance, health and endowment policies that offered the promise of financial security and lasting peace of mind.

Today, steadfastly maintaining a position attained in the days of Queen Victoria, the Prudential remains the UK's largest life assurer. But just as the hat has fallen out of favour as an item of corporate attire, so too has the Man from the Pru faded into distant memory.

In his place: ranks of headset-wearing agents in a computerized call centre; groups of brokers and intermediaries who swear allegiance to no single brand; and electronic forms for one-click submission on a company website.

In an age of instant networking and business-without-borders, the Prudential has radically altered its view of the world, expanding its interests to include a wide range of retail financial services in Europe, Asia and the USA. It's no longer just about protection against dread disease, disability and death.

Today, you can bank on a better tomorrow by setting aside money for everyday expenses, saving for the holiday or home of your dreams, or splashing out now and paying back in easy instalments later. But wait: what does life assurance have to do with retail banking? Why would you want to open a savings account, or apply for a credit facility, with the same company that sells you a ten-year endowment or a comprehensive income-protection plan?

In 1996, after more than a century of solid, prudent business in a field it had come to lead and define, the Prudential began asking itself the same kind of questions.

Here was a company that was paying out over £1 billion in maturing policies and arranging more than £700 million of mortgages through building societies each year. Here was a company with a client base of 6 million.

Six million individuals, with financial needs, goals and aspirations that stretched well beyond the boundaries of traditional insurance. Knock-knock. Who's there? The Man from the Pru. But this time, the knocking at the door was the sound of opportunity.

The answer, as it turned out, was a division called Prudential Banking plc, which would draw on the company's existing customer base and pave the way for a banking revolution.

A bank that didn't look like a bank, didn't sound like a bank, didn't feel like a bank. A bank called Egg.

It was a bank without branches; without sandstone pillars and marble lobbies; without tellers counting money behind plate-glass, or managers grimly considering overdrafts behind closed doors. All it had, to begin with, was an address in thin air: www.egg.com.

But from the moment it was made public, so many people began flocking to that address, that the very notion of banking as a bricks-and-mortar business would be shattered forever. The age of e-commerce had arrived, and the e stood for something that contained, within its fragile shell, the very essence of life itself. But before we crack it open, let's briefly click back to 1997.

Jim Sutcliffe, today Chief Executive of Old Mutual International, was at the time Chief Executive of Prudential in the UK, a position that included overall responsibility for the group's banking division, Prudential Banking plc.

The challenge, for Sutcliffe and his Board, was to "do something" with the division: to find a way of transforming and invigorating an entity that was widely perceived as little more than an afterthought to Prudential's core business.

Sutcliffe – facing off against the future

"It wasn't as if we were on a burning platform," recalls Sutcliffe. "Our traditional line of business was doing very well, thank you, but at the same time, we realized that the world around us was changing. We realized that we had to face off against the future."

Driven by that realization, Prudential was about to embark on a journey into a frontier where many businesses fear to tread. A frontier where the old rules and assumptions no longer apply, where long-established organizations and brands run the risk of being swallowed up by brash young upstarts.

And here's the really frightening thing:

the swallowing-up **happens from within.**

For today, it's **no longer good enough** simply to eat the competition. Today, you have to learn **to eat yourself.**

And Prudential Banking plc was about to be eaten...

by an upstart of its own creation.

As Sutcliffe recalls, the "self-cannibalization" of Prudential began with a growing awareness that the company was being overtaken by changing times and attitudes. While the venerable brand had lost none of its inherent warmth and integrity over the years, it was clearly out of touch with a younger, more cynical market: a growing core of consumers who had the money to buy, but would resist every attempt to be sold.

"It was a market we were very keen on," says Sutcliffe, "but we had to admit it was a market we didn't understand very well. If we were going to reach out to younger consumers – the big market of the future – we knew we were going to have to get out of the traditional box. We were going to have to think radical."

So well-entrenched and respected was the Prudential brand in the financial services sector, that the company could afford to break some rules and shatter some boundaries when it came to defining and capturing a niche in the retail banking market. With the full might of Prudential behind it, the new bank would instantly be seen as credible, stable and financially secure. It wouldn't have to prove a thing. Except perhaps…the reason for its own existence.

Weren't there already enough banks and building societies out there, scrambling for a share of the lucrative yet elusive "youth vote", with campaigns that included everything from discounted service charges to psychedelic credit cards to a free music CD of your choice on joining?

Big deal. The youth market, in more ways than one, wasn't buying.

Banks were seen as a necessary evil, a halfway house for the weekly wage-cheque, a convenient, impersonal channel for scoring cash from a machine outside the disco on a Saturday night. Could banks ever be hip? Could banks ever reflect the real lifestyles, real attitudes and real aspirations of the younger generation? You wouldn't want to bank on it.

"Our first attempts to get into the market were not at all successful," admits Sutcliffe. "To get a leg up into the retail market, we decided to partner with one of the UK's largest retail chains. But conflicts around which company would 'own' the information about the customer quickly brought the partnership to its knees. We decided that the Prudential would have to go it alone."

Goodbye discretion; farewell caution. What that decision entailed was a swift, complete and radical separation of the banking entity from its parent company. Behind the scenes, Prudential would still control the purse strings, but in every other sense, the new bank would be a fledgeling booted from the nest. It was going to have to learn to fly. And fast.

To give the as-yet-unnamed bank a hefty push into the limitless ether, Prudential called on one of its best men: Mike Harris, at the time CEO of Prudential Banking. The polar opposite of a traditional banking executive, Harris is a man with a relaxed demeanor and a natural, easygoing rapport with young and old.

On one memorable occasion, Harris took his staff out for a **team-building dinner.** But not for him, the stilted, formal confines of a five-star restaurant. Instead, the treat was a few filling courses at a local pie factory, with everyone singing bawdy rugby songs on the bus **there and back.**

Priority number one for Harris was "getting the culture right". Anyone who wanted to work for the new bank had to be saturated with its vibrant, upbeat, contemporary attitude. In other words, they had to believe – and live – a simple credo that banking could be fun. Your actual banking skills ran a very close second; they could always be worked on later. For now, what counted was the culture. And now, all that culture needed was a name.

As anyone who has ever been through the process will attest, naming a company or product is never quite as easy as it seems. With the help of corporate brand consultants, dozens of likely and not-so-likely contenders were weighed-up, analyzed and tossed around by the team charged with bringing the new bank to fruition.

The brief? Come up with a name that is "radically different, yet reassuringly familiar"; something that would mark a dazzling departure from the norm, while retaining at least a subliminal echo of the person-to-person values that made the original Man from the Pru such a trusted household name.

Among the early rejects: a simple, monosyllabic three-letter word that seemed to have very little to do with the world of financial products and services. Who ever heard of a bank called Egg? No-one. And that was precisely the point.

Despite the task team's formal rejection of the name, a junior staffer named Clive Wing began lobbying relentlessly on behalf of "Egg". Time and again, with unflagging passion and conviction, he tried to persuade the task team of its merits. He felt the name reflected just the right combination of emotional warmth, spontaneity and wit. On top of that, it was instantly catchy and easy to remember – all the more so for a generation not renowned for the length of its attention-span.

In a more traditional banking environment,
a junior staffer might have felt inclined to

"know his place"
and concede quickly and
with grace to
the views of his elders and betters.
But this wasn't a traditional banking environment.

With the maverick Mike Harris at the helm, this was a place where age and experience mattered less than energy and imagination. This was a place where leadership could come from anywhere. This was…what was that name again?

On 5 October 1998 the answer was revealed to the world. That was the day that Egg, initially hatched as a telephone bank, went live on the Internet, at www.egg.com. You could do your banking as and when you chose, wearing whatever you liked, performing every transaction at your own sweet pace, in your own sweet time. No tellers. No queues. No forms. Best of all, you could actually have fun while banking.

True, behind the flashy, funky website, with its catchy slogans, sunny-side-up graphics and step-right-in-and-feel-at-home ambience, there lay the powerful, finely-tuned engine of the old economy at its most familiar. A bank.

The interest rates, at least to begin with, may have been more generous, the loans more flexible, the products more cheerily-named. But it was a bank, all right. It just happened to be open for business on a different medium, with a different selling proposition in its favour. For this was a bank with attitude.

"We realized it would not be enough to simply offer cheaper and simpler products to our intended market," explains Sutcliffe. "To succeed, we were going to have to leap-frog all current thinking, and emerge with a radical new attitude towards banking.

"An attitude that wouldn't be perceived as too exclusive or too 'clever', but would appeal to the broadest possible mass of young customers. What was crucial, was that the new customer should perceive a complete shift from the traditional way of doing things."

And right from that opening day, thanks in large part to saturation advertising and the novelty of the proposition, the customer was there, flocking to the fledgeling financial institution at a rate that exceeded Egg's best-laid plans and ambitions. On day one, www.egg.com registered close to 1.75 million hits. But it wasn't just idle curiosity that drove the traffic.

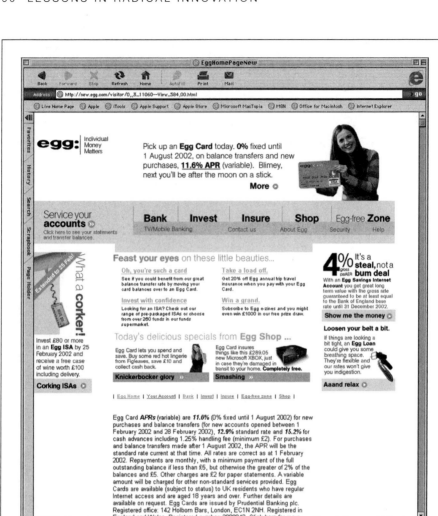

Egg on the web

According to Egg's original game plan, the bank was hoping to attract 400,000 active, paying customers within the first five years of operation. Instead, that figure was reached within seven months. By March 2001, the bank could boast 1.35 million customers and 1.75 million accounts. But for the old guard at Prudential, there was an even more pleasant surprise in store.

"Egg's appeal turned out to be much wider than we initially thought," says Sutcliffe. "A large part of the business came from an older customer base who, at an individual level, contributed far larger sums than our young target market!"

In retrospect, it wasn't too hard to divine the reasons for

Egg's across-the-board appeal.

One: you don't have to be young and trendy to feel disenchanted with traditional banks and banking.

Two: on the Internet, age doesn't matter.

It didn't take Egg long to learn that the way to build a thriving business on the Net is to build it through the power of a commodity more precious than gold, stocks or platinum. Relationships. With the DNA of a life assurance company in its genes, Egg instinctively knew the secrets of mining customer relationships for all they were worth.

And the Net, a purpose-built vehicle for building communities, forging links and replicating a message and a lifestyle through the power of multiple networks, was proving to be the motherlode for anyone in the customer-relationship business. As the number of customers grew, so did the number of possibilities for customizing the banking experience, and "cross-selling" a wide range of products and services in the process.

From its original set of offerings – little more than a channel for online trans-fers, payments and deposits – the Egg portfolio grew to encompass everything from credit cards to home loans to online shopping to travel insurance. More and more players began to be involved in creating the magic of innovation. Egg's Financial Director, Bob Head, led the creation of the UK's first "Investment Supermarket", offering a choice of 220 funds through 17 fund managers, for those seeking to build themselves a tidy little nest egg.

There was even a strictly-for-leisure section called "The Egg-Free Zone" and, in April 1999, seeking to broaden its appeal to the remaining mem-bers of the "off-line community", the bank launched its own ISP to provide unlimited free Internet access to anyone who wanted it.

And yet, as Egg was to discover, it's one thing to get the customer to buy into an irresistible proposition on the Internet; it's quite another to translate that proposition into profit.

In April 2000, Egg went public, with Prudential selling 20 per cent of its stake for £150 million. The timing couldn't have been worse. April turned out to be the cruellest month for global technology stocks, with the Nasdaq plunging massively on the very day of Egg's listing.

But unlike other eggs that had a great fall, Egg was able to rebound to the level of its opening share price (160p) within less than a year. It wasn't really an achievement worth crowing about and, as the years went by, the best Egg could do was point out that it was losing less money over time. In the third quarter of 2001, the bank recorded a pre-tax loss of just over £81 million, compared with £115 million for the same period in 2000. Boasting a healthy increase in customers and operating income, Egg could speak with some justification of the bank's "confident move towards profitability".

Happy birthday, dear smile...Bob Head celebrates in style

By the end of 2001, Egg had lost a total of £415 million. But it was in good company. Of its competitors, Cahoot had lost £120 million, while First-e had spent more than £130 million and then shut its doors. No-one ever said it was going to be cheap, or easy.

"The challenge constantly remains to make profits," says Jim Sutcliffe. "The costs of setting up the infrastructure are heavy, and once you're in business, you have to capitalize on satisfied customers by cross-selling as much as you can. Given the challenges, I think it's safe to say that Egg has done brilliantly well.

"It has set the pace
with a powerful new brand,
a distinctive attitude,
and a range of leading products."

But on a medium as hungry for novelty as the Internet, that's just the problem. No sooner have you set the pace, defined the attitude, and introduced the products, than other contenders ease themselves into the starting blocks, eager to undercut and overtake you by applying the lessons of your mistakes as much as your triumphs.

In October 1999, almost exactly a year after the launch of Egg, the battlefield of "bankless banking" heated up with the arrival of a new player: an Internet-only bank with a name designed to evoke an unfamiliar reaction among anyone accustomed to the drudgery of High Street banking.

Who ever heard of a bank called *smile*?
Once again, it seemed, just about
everybody.

Owned by Britain's Co-op group, the largest retail co-operative in the world, smile announced its arrival with a quick-loading

smile the internet bank

Going bananas... a novel promotion proves smile to be a master of mass appeal

website that featured blocks of blushing pink in the background. But there was more than just the look of lip-gloss to www.smile.co.uk.

Offering attractive interest rates, automatic overdrafts, special accounts for students, and a bold promise of exceptional customer service ("or we'll close your account for you"), smile recruited some 350,000 account-holders in its first 18 months, with 80 per cent of those customers coming from outside the existing Co-operative Bank.

With an infectious sense of fun and a fresh, witty approach to advertising its wares – in August 2001, smile began placing stickers with the bank's logo and the words TOP BANANA on each of the more than 150 million bananas sold at Co-op stores across Britain every year – smile swiftly made its mark in a fiercely competitive industry.

For three quarters in a row, between July 2000 and February 2001, smile was rated best online bank in the UK by Gomez, the respected, independent Internet assessment house. In an authoritative survey by *Which*, the magazine of the UK's notoriously hard-to-please Consumer Association, smile was rated best bank in any category. Industry and media commentators have hailed the bank for its simplicity, ease of access and over-riding emphasis on the personal touch.

If it sounds like Egg all over again, that's no wonder, for smile happens to be headed by a man named Bob Head, poached from his previous position as a founder and financial director of Egg. A breezy, down-to-earth maverick with an avowed distaste for accounting, Head flashes his trademark smile when asked how it feels to be in direct competition with his previous employer.

"Egg isn't the enemy," says the former Egghead, "traditional banks are the enemy! We're all on the same side – the side of the customer."

The smile principles

Value:	We'll provide or find deals to make your money go further
Transparency:	We won't hide extras anywhere and we'll tell you how we make a profit
Service:	We want you to love smile and we'll do everything in our power to keep you happy
Commerce:	We'll be honest with you and we'll campaign against companies who aren't
Ethical:	We'll be ethical and ecological because we're part of the Co-operative Bank
Accountable:	An independent customer panel will make sure we keep our promises and they'll tell you if we don't

It's an easy claim to make in a business environment where phrases like "customer-centric" and "customer service excellence" are tossed about with abandon, but Head is clearly a man who is prepared to put his money where his mouth is.

"Smile is a bank for people who are tired of the way banks have treated them in the past," he says. "It is a bank for people who have had enough of poor service and hidden surprises."

With this in mind, smile – the name is deliberately lower-case, to convey a sense of humility, friendliness and spontaneity – has adopted a set of unshakeable principles to live and breathe by.

What about security? Good question, answered by smile's proudly-proclaimed status as the only Internet bank in the UK to be awarded a BS7799 rating for Information Security Management Systems by the British Standards Institution.

But more than anything else, smile is driven by a simple determination to live up to its name. As Head puts it: "Work is all about having fun. It's about having a laugh – about not taking yourself too seriously. We call it the Monday Morning Test. If any of our staff don't feel like coming to work on Monday morning, then we have failed."

It's a simple point,
but Head hammers it home with emphasis.

If you want happy shareholders, if you want happy customers,
you've got to have happy people working for you.
That doesn't mean pasted-on smiles and forced conviviality.

It means "being", rather than "pretending".

"It's all about being honest and authentic," explains Head. "It's okay not to know something. In a lot of the stuff we are trying to do, there is no certainty, there are no precedents. We're doing things that have never been done before. In many cases, it's impossible to tell if we will succeed or not.

"That sort of thinking requires a radical new attitude to risk. If you want your staff to push the limits of what's possible in terms of customer value, you have to give them the permission to fail."

The upside of that approach is that people also have permission to succeed, to "allow their greatness to get out", as Head puts it. He talks about another test of corporate satisfaction as a measure of customer satisfaction: The Pub Party Test.

"When someone asks any of our employees who they work for, we want them to be able to say 'smile!' with pride and conviction – even in a pub. We want to build a business we can be proud of. We want our family and friends to know we work for the best online bank in the world – the best because our customers say so."

A chequebook with a smile

Behind the smile...the bank's call centre in operation

If all of this makes Bob Head sound satisfied with himself, his business and his workforce, forget it. He is the essence of the constantly dissatisfied entrepreneur, constantly turning radical thought into breakthrough action, constantly creating "focused turbulence" and being loved for it by customers and staff.

To Head, success flows from the application of a very simple formula, a pact between stakeholders, staff and customers. You begin by creating an environment in which staff are aligned, happy and fulfilled; in turn, they will create delighted customers. And there's nothing more powerful than that to meet and exceed the expectations of stakeholders.

So are smile's staff aligned, **happy and fulfilled?** They're more than that, beams Head. **They're an inspiration.** Proudly, he points out that **only six** of the bank's **200 employees** are paid more than £45,000 a year.

"Compare that to any other bank!" he exclaims. Smile's staff seem happy to do more than they're paid to do, with call-centre staff doubling as the testing team for new software releases, and others being intimately involved in the design process for new services.

Even when it comes to the simple matter of a company dress code, smile's staff defy the norms of a traditionally conservative industry. In most big organizations, frontline staff dress according to non-negotiable guidelines laid down in the company manual.

But when Bob Head arrived at smile, he offered call-centre staff the option of "dressing down" or wearing the suits to which all bankers are so well-accustomed.

"They thought about it," recalls Head, "and then they said, 'We don't want to dress down, and we don't want to wear suits.' I said, 'Well, we can't have a naked call centre!"

But that's not what the staff were thinking. They were thinking: we work for a bank called smile. And we want people to know that.

"They said, 'We want a uniform with smile branding on it – shirts, sweat-shirts, fleece, hat, bag'. So now that's we have. Except, we don't call it a uniform. We call it 'team togs'. It's a great leveller. If we get one customer conversion on the back of it per employee, then we are in the money. But the great thing is, it was not my idea. Leadership can come from anywhere."

Small wonder that smile is rated as one of the top 50 companies to work for in the UK. Considering that most of smile's customers are unlikely to ever have any face-to-face contact with the bank's staff, that palpable aura of personal, friendly service becomes all the more remarkable.

Head attributes it plainly to the fact that smile is a "no-bull" bank.

"What you see is what you get," he says. "We don't have branches, so the money we save on foyer plants and carpets goes towards paying customers over 30 times more interest than high street banks on a current account. It means we can charge you less when you're in debt – again, nearly half what you'd pay with a high street bank.

"How can we do this when other banks are trying to find ways to make more and more money? Simple. Unlike them, we're not quoted on the Stock Exchange – we're part of the Co-operative Movement."

Which is not to say that smile isn't at least partly in it for the money. Late in 2001, Co-operative Bank reported a before-tax profit of more than £60 million.

What puts a really big smile on Head's face is the fact that this was achieved with less than 10 per cent of the average marketing spend for an Internet bank.

"We probably spend less than **a quarter of the industry average on** systems development and testing. We really are **lean and mean.**"

Backed by innovative "guerrilla marketing" tactics – remember the smile stickers on the Co-op bananas – the bank moved swiftly towards its "viability" goal of 750,000 customers. In November 2001, two years after inception, smile was one of only three Internet-only banks to survive the dot com fallout in the UK.

The challenge now is not only to maintain that level of growth, but to maintain that level of leadership.

"When you're running such a lean organization," says Head, "you have to actively focus on building real leadership skills from within. A 'real banker' coming in to run this business would be a disaster! It would kill the spirit of the business."

For now, the business is thriving. As more and more customers choose to do their banking online, the initial concerns of poor security and daunting technology are being replaced by the joys of convenience, ease of access, and flexibility.

For Egg, smile and new contenders like Cahoot, the battle is hotting up, and it's likely that the victors will be decided not on the strength of their products, but on the strength of their relationships.

As Prudential's "Eggsperience" has proved, there's plenty of business – if not immediate profit – to be gained by smashing down traditional barriers, doing away with bricks and mortar, and placing a unique individual called "The Customer" at the core of the operation.

Still, this is the Internet, and what works today may not be what works tomorrow. Times and fortunes change, and even the most radically innovative first-mover can swiftly be forgotten in the onrush of a new and better way. For Egg, the company that hatched a revolution, the challenge is to stay ahead of its game – and if that means breaking the rules yet again, so much the better.

Towards the end of 2000, Egg announced plans to open a small number of bricks and mortar branches, not as an admission of defeat, but as an added convenience for customers who seek the best of both worlds: "high-touch", as well as high-tech. Who knows? Anything is possible.

Already, you can choose between banking online or banking in person. One day, your bank may even send the banker to you.

And when that happens,

the Man from the Pru

will finally have come full circle.

MY STRATEGIC ACTIONS?

Lessons learnt

Leaders create pain before the market does. Act before you have to. Act while you have a choice

Leadership can come from anywhere in the organization

In true innovation there are no precedents,
there is no certainty

Give people the permission to fail

Give people the space to grow and develop,
allow their greatness to emerge

Be authentic: give people something to be proud of

Victors will be decided not on the strength of their products,
but on the strength of their relationships.
Make relationship skills the first priority

Cannibalize your own business before someone else
does – own your new competitors

Lean + mean = profitable

Life's too short to stand in queues

We're all on the same side – the side of the customer

4

Breaking the mould

From workaday white to jungle green jalapeno

How Chef Works

re-wrote the global rules

for an industry and created the model of a fractal family business

In his office on the outskirts of Johannesburg, where the flyover leads to rows of run-down factories, warehouses, sporting arenas and semi-detached dwellings, Alan Gross clears some space on a table and throws down a pair of trousers.

They're made of cotton, with tapered legs, two side-pockets, and a draw-string round the waist. But those aren't the first things you notice. The first things you notice are the chilli peppers.

Red-hot, flame-orange, jungle-green.
Jalapeno, Pimiento, Banana.
You can almost taste the piquant tang, the

fiery zest that belies
the lightness of the fabric.

Then, just as your eyes are growing accustomed to the design, the trousers are whipped aside and replaced with another pair in the range.

This time, the flavour is Italian: plump tomatoes, sprigs of green onion, spaghetti twirled around a fork. A jazzy bouquet of colours, set against a deep charcoal background. There is the French look, with mushrooms, *escargot* and clumps of big black grapes. There is the Kitchen Utensils design, with its almost-audible clatter of chopping-knives, slicers and graters.

These are **not garments for the**
mild of heart,
the cautious of palate.

Even Alan Gross himself, young, upbeat and informal as he may be, would hesitate to wear them in public.

But that's not the point. The point is, they're flying off the shelves like…well, like, red-hot chilli peppers. "We just can't make them fast enough," says Gross, spinning around in his chair, leaning into his computer, clicking on the latest list of orders from the USA, Canada, England, Europe, Australia, New Zealand, Singapore, Japan, the Middle East and Africa.

The curious thing is, Gross isn't in the fashion business. He's not even in the food business. His territory lies somewhere in-between, in what he calls the fastest-growing niche in the fastest-growing industry in the world – the "hospitality clothing game".

Go to a restaurant, hotel or casino in almost any big city, and you probably won't notice what the chefs, the kitchen staff, the meeters-and-greeters are wearing. That's because they'll probably be wearing what people in their profession have been wearing for centuries: plain black or white outfits, crisply starched, with nothing more by way of embellishment than a discreetly-embroidered logo on the pocket.

But all that's changing. It's changing in a way that neatly encapsulates the shifting dynamics of business in the 21st Century: worlds in collision. E-commerce versus personalized, over-the-counter service. The small family enterprise versus the giant global franchise. A back-office on the southern tip of Africa versus a dot com on the web. Age-old tradition versus radical innovation.

Where does it all
begin?

Where does it lead? Where do you draw the line, how do you bridge the gulf?

How do you

leap-frog

the thinking

of others in your industry?

How do you change your way of doing business? How do you grow your market, without losing sight of the values and principles that built your business in the first place?

Today, it's a pair of funky baggies, a beanie hat, a baseball cap, an apron, a neckerchief or a doubled-breasted chef's jacket on www.chefwork.com. Yesterday, it was one man and his suitcase. Joseph Gross, son of Eastern European immigrants, hawking textiles door to door in the 1950s and 1960s, while his mother ran a little dress shop in the gold-rush city of Johannesburg.

The rag trade. If you're planning to accumulate riches, it's as good a place as any to start. One day, the customer says to the salesman: "I'm looking for a good, strong pair of overalls." It's not the salesman's line, but he smells an opportunity. He sub-contracts. The salesman becomes a middle-man. The customer is happy, the manufacturer is happy. In 1964, a brand-new business is born –

J. Gross & Co, suppliers and distributors of

a range of garments

that are as

practical and
functional as they are immune to
the shifting tides of trends.

Boilersuits, dustcoats, butchers' aprons, bakers' caps, overalls, safety boots, welding gloves. It's not high fashion, but it's a living.

By the mid-1970s, the family has grown as swiftly as the business. Five sons, one daughter. And yet, as the eldest son, Alan, leaves school and contemplates the long road ahead, there is no sign that he is getting ready to follow in his father's footsteps.

Academically lacklustre, headstrong and impulsive, he blazes his own trail, convincingly arguing his need to explore all possible options and prospects before he settles down to a career. The one thing he doesn't want to be, just because it's expected of him, is IDB – In Daddy's Business. So well does he put his case, that an acquaintance suggests, only half in jest: "You should be a lawyer."

So Alan Gross goes to Law School.
He lasts six
months.

Partly, it's because he's out on the street, chanting slogans, waving placards, protesting against the iniquity and inequity of the apartheid government that was then in power in South Africa. But the real reason has very little to do with politics.

Alan Gross: "The one thing I am is totally wound. And I can talk."

Looking back from the distance of his more sedate 40s, he readily admits that he lacked the legal mind to match his legal mouth. He talks at the pace of a runaway train, switching tracks in mid-thought, drumming his fingers on the table, glancing around the room, barely able to sit still for a minute. He wouldn't have lasted long in court.

"I never was any great shakes at school or university," says Gross. "I have this thing, I can't concentrate on reading. I probably should have been on Ritalin. But put me in front of a computer, and I can do anything. The one thing I am, is totally wound. I have enormous amounts of energy. And I can talk."

As it would turn out, it was precisely that combination – a short attention-span, a restless, inquisitive nature, a non-linear way of thinking, a rebellious streak and a natural ability to communicate – that would prove to be the springboard for J. Gross & Co's quantum jump into the future.

But even after dropping out of his law degree and completing his year of military service, then an obligation for every able-bodied white South African male, Alan Gross still felt no inclination to get into workwear and protective clothing. An uncle offered him a job at a garage in Johannesburg. Maybe he could try working with his hands. "I burned my hands on a whole lot of exhaust pipes," sighs Gross.

"My father said, 'Come. It's time you learned the game.'"

In 1977, a new dispatch clerk joined the small team at J. Gross & Co. Alan Gross's job was to make sure all the paperwork was in order before the boiler-suits, safety boots and blood-and-fat-resistant butchers' capes went out the door. For someone who can't sit still for a minute, it must have been torment.

Gross knew, if he was going to survive in the family business, that his future wasn't going to lie in dispatch. He was going to have to get out there, into the market, and do what he did best: win friends and influence people. As the company's new sales director, he pushed the boundaries by selling workwear and protective clothing in such neighbouring African territories as Zambia, Botswana, Malawi, Angola, Mozambique and Uganda.

For generations, family businesses have served as models of the best and worst in business practice.

South Africa's apartheid-enforced isolation made it difficult to push the boundaries any further, but J. Gross & Co was changing in other ways as well. By buying a bankrupt clothing factory in the coastal city of Durban, the business was able to add the missing link to its chain of value: manufacturing, supply and distribution. Now, it was all in the business. Now, it was all in the family.

For generations, across the world, family businesses have served as models of the best and worst in business practice.

On the one hand, by establishing lines of succession, they provide a welcome sense of continuity and security through the ages. Where there is conflict – and no dynasty can count itself immune from conflict – resolution is often more swiftly reached around the dining-table than in the courtroom.

By tradition, the family business

embodies warmth, trust, and goodwill, which find their outlet in personalized service and a hands-on, no-nonsense management style.

Decisions can be swiftly made, plans quickly put into action.

On the other hand, a family business can be insular and parochial, suspicious of outsiders, and seemingly oblivious to the flaws and weaknesses of those family members who may not have earned their positions on merit alone.

But in many cases, the dominant negative gene in a family business is the very thing that otherwise ensures its stability...

PRINTED BASEBALL CAPS
CASQUETTES DE BASEBALL À IMPRIMÉ $16.00

PEPPER | ITEM BBPP
POIVRE | ARTICLE BBPP

CHEF PRINT | ITEM BBCP
IMPRIMÉ CHEF | ARTICLE BBCP

FRENCH | ITEM BBFR
FRANÇAISE | ARTICLE BBFR

ITALIAN | ITEM BBIT
ITALIENNE | ARTICLE BBIT

BLACK/NOIR
| ITEM BBBC

WHITE/BLANC
| ITEM BBWT

CHALK STRIPE | ITEM BBCS
À RAYURES BLANC DE CRAIE
| ARTICLE BBCS

BARBED WIRE | ITEM BBBW
FIL DE FER BARNELÉ
| ARTICLE BBBW

KNIVES | ITEM BBKN
COUTEAUX | ARTICLE BBKN

FISH | ITEM BBFI
POISSONS | ARTICLE BBFI

SMALL CHECK | ITEM BBCH
PITITS CARREAUX | ARTICLE BBCH

ROYAL CUISINE | ITEM BBCC
ROYAL CUISINE | ARTICLE BBCC

UTENSILS | ITEM BBUT
USTENSILES | ARTICLE BBUT

CHEF HATS $15,95
ONE SIZE FITS ALL, VELCRO CLOSE AT THE BACK
TOQUES DE CHEF
UNITAILLE, FERMETURE AJUSTABLE EN VELCRO À L'ARRIÈRE

SKULL CAPS $14,95
EXPANDABLE ELASTIC BACK
CALOTTES
PARTIE ÉLASTIQUE À L'ARRIÈRE

BERETS $15,95
ONE SIZE FITS ALL, ADJUSTABLE DRAWSTRING WITH AIR VENTS
BÉRETS
UNITAILLE, CORDON AJUSTABLE A VEC OUVERTURES DE VENTILATION

BLACK | ITEM BHAT
NOIRE | ARTICLE BHAT

SMALL CHECK | ITEM CHBW
PETITS CARREAUX
| ARTICLE CHBW

FISH | ITEM FICH
POISSONS | ARTICLE FICH

WHITE | ITEM CHAT
BLANC | ARTICLE CHAT

CHALK STRIPE | ITEM CSCH
À RAYURES BLANC DE CRAIE
| ARTICLE CSCH

UTENSILS | ITEM UTCH
USTENSILES | ARTICLE UTCH

CUISINE BLACK | ITEM BOCH
CUISINE NOIRE | ARTICLE BOCH

KNIVES | ITEM KNCH
COUTEAUX | ARTICLE KNCH

BARBED WIRE | ITEM BWCH
FIL DE FER BARBELÉ
| ARTICLE BWCH

CUISINE BLUE | ITEM CUCH
CUISINE BLEUE | ARTICLE CUCH

BLACK | ITEM SCBL
NOIRE | ARTICLE SCBL

WHITE | ITEM SCWH
BLANCHE | ARTICLE SCWH

PEPPER | ITEM SCPP
POIVRE | ARTICLE SCPP

FRENCH | ITEM SCFR
FRANÇAISE | ARTICLE SCFR

SMALL CHECK | ITEM SCSC
PITITS CARREAUX | ARTICLE SCSC

ITALIAN | ITEM SCIT
ITALIÉNNE | ARTICLE SCIT

BLACK | ITEM BEBL
NOIR | ARTICLE BEBL

WHITE | ITEM BEWH
BLANC | ARTICLE BEWH

PEPPER | ITEM BEPP
POIVRE | ARTICLE BEPP

BARBED WIRE | ITEM BEBW
FIL DE FER BARBELÉ
| ARTICLE BEBW

SMALL CHECK | ITEM BESC
PETITS CARREAUX
| ARTICLE BESC

ITALIAN | ITEM BEIT
ITALIEN | ARTICLE BEIT

24

Chef Works…radically changing the face of kitchen couture

Resistance to change.

In the case of J. Gross & Co, there was a constant clash between the father's inherent conservatism, and the eldest son's aggressive, "get-out-there" approach to sales and marketing.

It wasn't so much a clash of wills, as a clash of styles. Here was a company that had slowly, painstakingly earned itself a comfortable niche in a difficult and overtraded industry. But for Alan Gross, a position of national leadership in workwear and protective clothing was not, when you thought about it, that much of a big deal. South Africa was small, distant, off the map.

There had to be other markets out there, other opportunities.

In 1994, when South Africa finally made its transition from apartheid to democracy, the door to the outside world began opening. And Gross was ready, as always, to put his foot in it.

On a family vacation in Washington DC, tired of malls, monuments and museums, he picked up a copy of the *Yellow Pages* and looked under chefs' clothing. It was a line that made up only 20 per cent of the J. Gross inventory, which seemed to leave a lot of room for expansion. Anyway, what harm could there be in checking out the competition? Yes, there were some big and established suppliers of clothing to the hospitality industry. Yes, the quality and the prices were good. Yes, it was going to be hard, for a small company from South Africa to break in and get a slice of the market. But you couldn't argue with the arithmetic. In Las Vegas alone, there are more than 160,000 hotel beds. In the whole of South Africa, maybe 75,000. And let's not even talk about the restaurants.

Gross, the family businessman, started calling on his connections. There was younger brother Dale, a "whizzkid" insurance marketer, who had previously emigrated to America and was now working in the telecommunications industry. There was a cousin of Adele Gross, Alan's ever-supportive wife, who happened to be a successful software developer in the USA. Just by coincidence, his portfolio included a hospitality industry clothing management program.

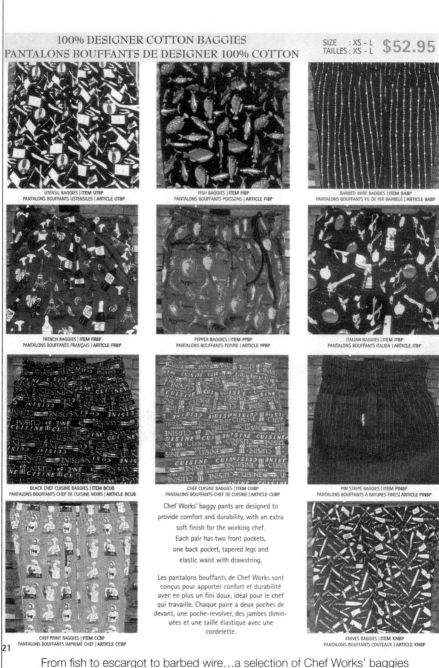

100% DESIGNER COTTON BAGGIES
PANTALONS BOUFFANTS DE DESIGNER 100% COTTON

SIZE : XS - L
TAILLES : XS - L **$52.95**

UTENSIL BAGGIES | ITEM UTBP
PANTALONS BOUFFANTS USTENSILES | ARTICLE UTBP

FISH BAGGIES | ITEM FIBP
PANTALONS BOUFFANTS POISSONS | ARTICLE FIBP

BARBED WIRE BAGGIES | ITEM BABP
PANTALONS BOUFFANTS FIL DE FER BARBELÉ | ARTICLE BABP

FRENCH BAGGIES | ITEM FRBP
PANTALONS BOUFFANTS FRANÇAIS | ARTICLE FRBP

PEPPER BAGGIES | ITEM PPBP
PANTALONS BOUFFANTS POIVRE | ARTICLE PPBP

ITALIAN BAGGIES | ITEM ITBP
PANTALONS BOUFFANTS ITALIEN | ARTICLE ITBP

BLACK CHEF CUISINE BAGGIES | ITEM BCUB
PANTALONS BOUFFANTS CHEF DE CUISINE NOIRS | ARTICLE BCUB

CHEF CUISINE BAGGIES | ITEM CUBP
PANTALONS BOUFFANTS CHEF DE CUISINE | ARTICLE CUBP

PIN STRIPE BAGGIES | ITEM PINBP
PANTALONS BOUFFANTS À RAYURES FINES| ARTICLE PINBP

Chef Works' baggy pants are designed to
provide comfort and durability, with an extra
soft finish for the working chef.
Each pair has two front pockets,
one back pocket, tapered legs and
elastic waist with drawstring.

Les pantalons bouffants de Chef Works sont
conçus pour apporter confort et durabilité
avec en plus un fini doux, idéal pour le chef
qui travaille. Chaque paire a deux poches de
devant, une poche-revolver, des jambes dimin-
uées et une taille élastique avec une
cordelette.

CHEF PRINT BAGGIES | ITEM CCBP
PANTALONS BOUFFANTS IMPRIMÉ CHEF | ARTICLE CCBP

KNIVES BAGGIES | ITEM KNBP
PANTALONS BOUFFANTS COUTEAUX | ARTICLE KNBP

21

From fish to escargot to barbed wire…a selection of Chef Works' baggies

Employees would check-in for work, hand in their civilian clothes, and swipe a card through a machine. A conveyer belt would bring them their uniforms, which would have small electronic transponders fused into the material. At the end of the shift, the process would be repeated in reverse, controlled all along by computers and a piece of custom-designed software.

Connections were made. Together with Dale, Alan met with the sales manager of a major American distributor of hospitality clothing. He liked what he saw. He flipped through the catalogue, felt the cut of the material. He looked at Gross. "How many containers a week can you ship?"

Gross gulped.

For once putting the reins on his global ambitions, he agreed to send a single container of mixed hospitality outfits, from chefs' jackets to waiters' tunics to maids' aprons, as a test of the American market.

Three months passed. Hardly a single item shifted.

Faced with a container-full of crisply-starched outfits that nobody wanted, Gross began questioning not just his judgment, but his very understanding of the business he was in. It wasn't the fashion game. That was the whole point. You're selling workwear. You're not selling something that's going to go out of style or flavour just because somebody in Paris says so.

Sitting in his office in Johannesburg, Gross gestures at rows and rows of garments shrouded in plastic, ready for dispatch.

"There's not a dead item in that warehouse," he says. "You won't find last year's bellbottoms or last year's miniskirt. Every item in there is going to get sold, if not this month, then next month or the month after. It's a staple, like the sugar in your kitchen. It may not go as fast, but with the laundries washing hell out of the garment, and adding chlorine bleach to it, you're going to have to replace it sooner or later."

You live by volume, not by margins. You can't afford to become a victim of fashion. And yet, if you're selling to people in the restaurant and hotel trade, you're selling, by definition, to people at the cutting-edge of trend. People with the power to dictate public taste, to define the flavour of the month. Who says you can't play the game by the same rules?

Let's take the standard, classic chef's jacket, for example. Who says it has to be 100 per cent cotton, 100 per cent white?

Why can't it be denim and blue? Why can't it be black? Why can't an executive chef in one of the world's top restaurants go to work in a pair of brightly-coloured, chilli pepper-printed baggies, as long as they're comfortable, practical and in line with all the relevant local health regulations?

Who says you can't look like you're having fun, just because you're working in the kitchen?

Already, on TV, you've got guys like Keith Floyd, sipping wine as he whips up exotic dishes in exotic locations, and Jamie Oliver, the Naked Chef, with his wild hair and his wild shirts and his hot 'n spicy "pukka tukka" cuisine.

No wonder that container in the States isn't shifting.

Ahead of the pack…top chefs sporting Chef Works' beanies

"If we were going to break into the American market," recalls Alan Gross, "we were going to have to reinvent ourselves. We were going to have to get into the funky and outrageous stuff that the celebrity chefs were wearing. It was a bit of a culture shock for us. My father said, 'Look, we're not fashion people. We're in workwear. Do we really want to get involved in this?' But that's the way the market was moving. That was our opportunity."

Soon, the opportunity is seized and transformed into an independent American distribution company called Chef Works, run from America by Dale Gross and two of his brothers: Clive, who used to run a small clothing company in South Africa, and Neil, formerly operations director of J. Gross & Co in Johannesburg.

The idea is that J. Gross & Co will manufacture a specialized line of chef's clothing and ship it to Chef Works, who will get the goods moving in the American market. But first, someone has to design the funky and outrageous stuff. Clive volunteers.

He draws his inspiration, as chefs themselves do, from the things that make life worth living. Good food. Good wine. Good spices. Good sauce. To tell the truth, not everyone shares his taste.

Back in Johannesburg, Alan and Joe Gross are

looking at chilli peppers and pasta

and fish and mushrooms.

On workwear. On trousers
and aprons and beanie hats.

They're scratching their heads.

Who's going to want to
wear this stuff?

It's 2002. Chef Works has more than 30,000 customers in the American market alone. It's the preferred supplier to two major hotel groups. It supplies casinos, cruise lines, restaurants.

Go to Tavern on the Green in New York. Go to Pampelmousse in San Diego. Go to Maloney & Porcelli, go to Rain, go to the St Regis or the Hilton or the Hotel Del Coronado. What's the Executive Chef wearing? What's the Sous Chef wearing? What's the Pastry Chef wearing? Chef Works.

"It's been amazing to me," says Alan Gross. "That we as a South African company could even think of selling our goods overseas. I mean, we're a mature South African business. We always thought we'd be able to make a living, and educate our children. We always thought we understood the boundaries.

Suddenly, the whole picture changes radically. Suddenly, we're global. Suddenly, everything's different."

Gross is walking through the family warehouse in Johannesburg. He casts a quick, practised eye over the goods that built the business: boilersuits, overalls, combat trousers, PVC raincoats. They're still here, they still sell. But now, they're outsourced. Now, the full manufacturing capacity of the J. Gross & Co plant is devoted to hospitality clothing by Chef Works. Now, the containers are shifting.

The biggest lessons: if you want to move the goods, try to cut out the middleman. Shorten the distance between yourself and the customer. Focus your business on the things that set you apart.

In 1997, inspired to get wired, Gross persuades his brothers that the time has come to turn Chef Works into a dot com. The company is about to launch its first major catalogue in the USA. Gross, an early Internet adapter, believes the site should be more than just a "banner-waving" exercise. He wants something that will add to the bottom line. He wants a viable, easy-to-manage e-commerce portal.

Alan wants Chef Works to be
the Amazon.com
of the hospitality clothing industry.

With the backing of his American-based brothers, Gross commissions a South African Internet company to build the site. They build something, but it's not what Gross wants. They try again. Increasingly frustrated, Gross does what he should have done in the first place. He sources from within.

The other Gross brother, Gerald, is a computer programmer based in Europe. Websites aren't really his line. He's more into databases. But that's exactly the point: if you can manage the information about your customers, you can manage the customers. And if you can build on those customer relationships, then you're in business.

If you're starting something new,
you have to build your business
around the customer!

You also have to build alliances with business partners who can add real value to the customer relationship. Take the vital business of shipping, for instance. Today, www.chefwork.com has in excess of 100,000 garments in stock in the USA alone, and any item can be shipped to its destination within 24 hours of order.

Chef Works sources its shipping through a partnership with UPS and it's not just about automating the shipping of goods. UPS have become an integral part of their warehousing and logistics. They have installed their automated scales and bar code printers inside the Chef Works warehouse. Customers can track their shipments online using UPS's advanced systems.

UPS began offering their customers the ability to track parcels on the web in 1995. At first they didn't understand what all the fuss was about or why any customer would want to do that, considering their proud record of on-time delivery.

For customers too, tracking parcels has become the norm. From less than 600,000 people checking on their deliveries by phone just five years ago, today more than 4 million UPS customers a day now track their parcels via the Internet. And that figure includes many of Chef Works customers.

Not content with handling the 13 million packages per day, UPS will take over your entire e-commerce operation should you not want to do that in-house. They will provide warehousing space and manage your inventory. In fact, they will mange the entire logistics process for your business. Through UPS Capital they will even take some credit risk and handle payments for you.

Any business, no matter what size, can capitalize on these fractal resources to tie in to the world's best logistics skills, from wherever they are. You can source anything from anywhere – even though your choice of business partners for truly global logistics is quite limited. You won't find much beyond UPS, FedEx and DHL.

But the true scope of your fractal
business is limited only by

the quality of your thinking.

Today, www.chefwork.com accounts for some 20 per cent of the company's American business.

And it's not just the hospitality industry that's doing the buying.

"I think a lot of it is people who just like to wear chilli pepper baggies," says Gross. "That's the beauty of the Internet. You get some guy in Biloxi, Mississippi, who would never otherwise be your customer, and here he is placing an order because your site comes up in his search engine."

It's the best of all possible worlds. The customer from the Congo, calling to collect his special delivery of boilersuits at the counter of J. Gross & Co. in Johannesburg. The customer from Biloxi, clicking to complete his order for a pair of Italian baggies. The handshake at the trade show. The e-mail from across the world. The real and the virtual. The bricks and the clicks.

"This isn't a boo.com," says Gross, referring to the super-hip online clothing retailer that spectacularly ran out of steam and money in 2000. "This is a solid manufacturing company with stocks and debtors. We're still cumbersome in many ways. We've been in business for almost 40 years, and two generations. But at the same time, we're only just beginning."

The thing is, it's still a family business. Except now, the family's gone global and fractal.

It's a model of a vibrant new style of business: the fractal organization. Unbounded by geography, unrestricted by hierarchy, drawing its strength and inspiration from a common gene pool of old-fashioned values and service to the customer.

Neil and Dale and Clive in America, running the company, taking the orders, designing the goods. Gerald in Europe, managing the database, coding the HTML. Alan in Johannesburg, still trying to do everything at once. Joe Gross, the founding father, still measuring the cut of the cloth, still feeling the quality, still selling the finest workwear and protective clothing in the business.

Hot-footing his way through the warehouse, Alan Gross suddenly pulls to a halt, reaches up to a shelf and rips open a covering of clear plastic. He pulls out a beanie hat and puts it on his head. It's the latest in the range. This time, no food or utensils in the design. Just a few thin, silvery strands against a black background.

"Barbed wire," says Gross. "Inspired by South Africa."

It's a playful jibe at the mood of a paranoid nation, hiding its fears behind burglar bars, high walls and security alarms. But look beyond, and you'll see that things are changing radically.

The fences are down, the boundaries are gone.

The world is the territory.

Alan Gross smiles and puts the beanie back on the shelf. After all, somebody out there is waiting for it.

MY IDEAS FOR THE FUTURE ?

Lessons learnt

Check that the definition of "your business" doesn't limit your future markets

Focus on what really differentiates you

What is your core competence? Design?

Outsource the traditional business if it has become commoditized

Cut out the middleman

Business is a fractal network without geography

Who says a chef's uniform has to be white?

Question every existing rule

Thirty years of evolutionary growth
can be eclipsed by five years of radical innovation

5

Choosing intimacy

Beyond operational efficiency and product leadership

How Denmark's IHI is re-writing the rules of customer service in global markets, putting its customers at the centre of the value network

There is an island off the southeast coast of Africa, where the trade winds bring rain and the occasional cyclone, and jagged peaks of black volcanic rock soar above fields of sugarcane and the blue-fringed coral reefs of the warm Indian Ocean.

The tourist brochures call this place Paradise on Earth; the locals know it better as Mauritius. If you look at a map of the world, Mauritius will be the small dot to the right of Madagascar.

Now draw a line from the dot, cutting your way across the highlands of Ethiopia, the deserts of Sudan and Egypt, the Mediterranean Sea, the even tinier dots that cluster like shrapnel off the coast of Greece, up through the heart of Europe until you reach Copenhagen, capital city of the Kingdom of Denmark.

It is 1972. You have just followed the flight path of a letter posted in Port Louis, and bearing the address of the head office of one of the largest insurance companies in Scandinavia, the Sygeforsikringen Danmark.

The stamp on the envelope, vibrantly-coloured, reflecting the plumes of a bird found only in these tropical climes, would not draw a second glance anywhere in Mauritius. But here, thousands of kilometres away, on the edge of the icy Baltic Sea, with its archipelago of 483 mostly uninhabited islands, it immediately catches the eye of an amateur philatelist named Per Bay Jorgenson.

Jorgenson picks up the envelope, studies the stamp, makes a mental note to steam it off and add it to his collection. Then he opens the letter, because that is part of his job.

A computer specialist by training, he works in the processing department of the Sygeforsikringen Danmark, known to staff and clients alike simply as the Danmark.

Per Bay Jorgenson

And this is a letter from a client. A client on the other side of the world; a client of the most troublesome kind. A client with a complaint.

The expatriate Dane, a sea-pilot living and working in Mauritius, has written to express concern at the fact that he is no longer entitled to receive health insurance benefits from the Danish government, thanks to recent reforms of the country's health and social welfare legislation.

True, the Danes have always enjoyed one of the highest standards of living in the world, with free and compulsory education, generous pension pay-outs and free and compulsory health insurance coverage. But what about Danes living outside Denmark?

Suddenly, Per Bay Jorgenson isn't thinking about the pretty stamp on the envelope. Suddenly, he's thinking of all the Danes, all over the world, who will have to dip into their own pockets the next time they are bitten by a tsetse-fly, or poisoned by beri-beri, or struck by a fast-moving vehicle travelling on the wrong side of the road. This isn't a crisis, thinks Jorgenson. This is an opportunity. He goes to see his manager.

Fast-forward to the present day. The stamp collection of Per Bay Jorgenson has grown by leaps and bounds. Colourful and exotic specimens from the

THE WORLD IS YOUR PLAYGROUND. There are no limitations and every possibility is within reach. No matter when or where, you only settle for the best. Particularly when it comes to your health, you want to secure yourself and your family, so you can enjoy life wherever you are.

International Health Insurance is dedicated to offering you a health plan, which gives you superior worldwide medical cover. It protects you and your family for life, regardless of where you live or travel.

WE ARE WITH YOU EVERYWHERE

Name

Address

Postal Code   City

Country   Tel:

E-mail   Age   Nationality

Choice of Currency   ☐ GBP   ☐ EURO   ☐ USD   ☐ DKK

Send the coupon to: International Health Insurance danmark a/s
Denmark: Palaegade 8, DK-1261 Copenhagen K, Tel: +45 33 15 30 99, Fax: +45 33 32 25 60
Isle of Man: 64a Athol Street, Douglas, Isle of Man, British Isles IM1 1JE, Tel: +44 1624 677412, Fax: +44 1624 675856

International Health Insurance danmark a/s

TO KNOW MORE, JUST CALL +45 33 15 30 99, VISIT WWW.IHI.DK OR SEND THE COUPON

IHI's omnipresent promise…"We are with you everywhere"

furthest reaches of the planet: Bolivia, Uzbekistan, Tonga, French Polynesia. But that's nothing. For the real core of Jorgenson's world, the real stamp of his success, is a company that can trace its origins back to that single letter, from that single Dane living abroad.

International Health Insurance, or IHI. Founded as a fully-owned subsidiary of Sygeforsikringen Danmark in 1979, with Jorgenson as CEO, IHI has grown from three employees to over 300, and from 300 customers to over 300,000, with an average annual growth rate of 25 per cent in earnings. The company is seen by many as a role model of radical innovation in its field, and has even been the subject of an in-depth business study by the management school of London's Imperial College, under Professor Sandra Vandermerwe. Through all the growth, IHI's market remains fundamentally the same: expatriates – retirees, emigrants, contract workers, travellers – requiring private health cover while abroad.

But the not-so-simple thing about IHI is **the way that small niche has been transformed into** the basis of a global business empire, **in defiance of** every conventional wisdom that governs the field of health insurance. "From the outset," recalls Jorgenson, **"we wanted our company to** be **radically different** from any of its competitors."

Insurance is a numbers game. The bottom line lies in the art of balancing the number of policies sold, with the number of claims paid. In order to get that

right, you have to price your products aggressively: everyone knows insurance is the ultimate grudge purchase, and the only sure way to lessen that grudge is to offer lower premiums and better benefits than the other guys.

So how come, if you want to take out a health insurance policy with IHI, you're expected to pay twice, three times, four times more than the other guys will charge you? (Example: if you're a 30-year-old male, William Russell will sell you a policy for a premium of £536. Go to IHI, and you'll wind up paying £2087.)

The answer lies in the single word on which the world of modern business turns.

Value.

"Traditional insurance companies have always put the focus on price," says Jorgenson. "We decided to put the focus on service and customer intimacy. That meant offering better, more relevant products and charging a premium for them, on the basis that our customers would save time, money, hassle and stress over the long term."

It helped that the customers in IHI's target market were, by nature, a group of people capable of taking the long view on price versus value. They were high-income earners, typically ambitious and entrepreneurial, often with homes in two or more countries, who simply wanted to rest assured that they would be covered for treatment of the highest possible standard, should any illness or accident befall them while abroad.

Initially focusing on Danish expatriates, IHI soon began offering its products to expatriates of all nationalities, the common thread being the choice and flexibility of a comprehensive health insurance package, which would cover everything from dental and medical treatment through emergency evacuation to major surgery.

Policyholders would be able to consult the medical professionals of their choice, anywhere in the world, with bills for hospital stays being sent directly to IHI, and expenses being reimbursed in whatever currency was required.

Complete coverage and freedom of choice were the **watchwords,** communicated through a hard-hitting campaign in glossy expatriate journals and international newspapers.

As a global brand, IHI soon began holding the same cachet as Rolls Royce or Gucci: purveyors of luxury items that are not necessarily regarded as luxuries by those who can afford them. Money may not buy you happiness; it may not even be able to buy you health. But it can buy you a priceless commodity called peace of mind, with the promise of superior service into the bargain.

Since it is only really put to the test in the worst of times – illness, robbery, natural disaster – insurance is, at least in theory, the most service-oriented and customer-centric industry of them all. But anyone who has ever been bounced from claims clerk to claims clerk, or battled to make sense of a sub-clause on a policy document, will understand that it doesn't always work that way in practice.

The problem, believes Jorgenson, is that insurance companies put too much emphasis on policies, and not enough on people. "Most companies are geared towards the average customer in everything they do," he says. "They're inflexible when it comes to the individual needs of individual people."

IHI, on the other hand, can trace its very origin to the needs of one individual – a Danish sea-pilot living on a faraway island off the southeast coast of Africa. But that Dane has given way to a diverse community of nationalities and cultures, and that island has grown to encompass the world.

Even so, for all its global reach, IHI retains the air of a company where "customer intimacy" has always been the guiding principle. As more and more expatriates bought into the concept of "complete coverage and freedom of choice", IHI began setting up branches and contracting intermediaries in territories as far afield as Spain, Bolivia, Japan, France and the Isle of Man.

Ubiquitous and cosmopolitan...an IHI ad sums up the company's global reach

For Jorgenson, the goal wasn't simply to establish a physical presence in expatriate markets. The goal was to serve the customer. Not as easy as it sounds, particularly when you're dealing with a range of different languages, different attitudes, different cultures.

"The difference between markets demands a distinct approach in each country, so as to suit local conditions and cultural norms," he says. "It was vital for us to set up operating and delivery systems that would be consistent with the service levels for which we were known."

The secret: act globally, think locally.

In each chosen market – entry being based on a critical mass of at least $2 million worth of potential contributions to the portfolio – IHI would set up a small branch, typically with a staff of three, well-versed in the local language and the local culture. This would be the frontline of IHI's customer service strategy: people talking to people, face to face, cutting through the barriers of legalese and bureaucracy.

If you fell ill while abroad, you'd be able to make use of IHI's own extensive database of approved hospitals and medical consultants around the world. You'd be able to call an IHI hotline, 24 hours a day, seven days a week, for advice and support. You'd even get a visit, if required, from an IHI-contracted health professional who spoke your language.

This was service; this was value. The rest, in Jorgenson's view, could be taken care of by technology. Each of the small satellite branches would be connected to the central office in Copenhagen, providing the backbone for a more efficient, more streamlined, more cost-effective way of doing business.

It's one of the great ironies of our age: if you want to offer your customers personalized service, ease of access and the swiftest possible response to their individual needs, you have to do it in a way that reduces the level of direct contact with human beings. You have to do it by computer.

With his own background in information technology, stretching way back to before it was even called information technology, Jorgenson was quick to adapt his company to the possibilities of a new channel, a new medium, for speeding up the processes at the core of health insurance.

IHI was one of the first companies in
its field to harness the power of
the Internet as something more than
a platform for marketing its products and services.
For the company's well-off,
well-connected client base,
it made perfect
sense to peruse the brochures, dip into
the financials,
apply for cover, and submit claims online.

Has that meant a shift in focus away from more traditional notions of customer service? Far from it. Many companies take pride in declaring that customer service is their obsession; in reality, it's more often an afterthought, even an irritation. The real obsession is the bottom line.

But for Jorgenson, it's impossible to separate the two. Customer service IS the bottom line. For the CEO, that means getting out into the market, being the "face" of the company, listening to suggestions, offering advice, dealing with problems, talking to staff, policyholders, partners, intermediaries and medical professionals in every territory where IHI has a presence.

It also means finding the right people: people who share that obsession, people who understand the business, people who know that the art of effective communication begins with the ability to listen.

In the culture of IHI, it's taken for granted that customer service may be needed most when the customer is sick, nervous or upset; consequently, anyone who works for the company is expected to be "a shining sun over the phone", ready and able to ease the crisis by helping to find the solution.

In contrast with many other insurance companies, staffers at IHI are much more than "stampers of forms". They're often university graduates, fluent in English and at least one other language (Spanish, French, German, Italian) as well as their mother tongue.

They're expected to be capable of thinking on their feet and making quick, "real-time" decisions, based on individual circumstances rather than standardized, by-the-book procedure. Not surprisingly, such staffers are hard to come by, and they're especially unlikely to be found in more traditional insurance organizations.

At IHI, for instance, there are no separate, dedicated service teams to handle underwriting and claims. It's easier to run an insurance company that way, admits Jorgenson; but it's also the height of drudgery and tedium for staff.

"We would lose 50 per cent of our people if we did it that way. It would just be too boring for them, and the customer would not get a seamless experience."

So at IHI, people learn to multi-task. Service teams are organized along strictly regional lines, ensuring that customers are never shunted from division to division, and allowing staff to gain a more realistic overview of company systems and procedures in the process.

"They see money going in and money going out," says Jorgenson. "In other companies claims people will only see money going out, so their natural reaction is to say 'no', to delay it as long as possible."

To hasten the process at IHI, checking and double-checking of figures has largely been eliminated in favour of individual approval limits, which are set according to a staff-member's position in the company. Students have the lowest limit; Jorgenson the highest.

"The object is to pay claims quickly," he explains. "If you can't do that, customers are mad as hell, and none of the other services will matter."

It's all about a

seamless customer
experience.

What matters at IHI, plain and simple, is the basic commodity on which the company has been built. Never mind the intricacies of individual insurance cover, designed for different individuals in different parts of the world. The commodity in question is customer service.

Just ask that Danish sea-pilot, who probably expected nothing more than a polite form-letter in response to his complaint about the side effects of a government edict.

Instead, he got a company that saw the gap, seized the initiative, and grew to lead the expatriate health insurance market, all because one young man, far away in Copenhagen, took the trouble to read the letter that lurked behind a colourful stamp.

In truth, that was the easy bit.

"It's quite easy to build and establish an insurance company," insists Jorgenson. "The challenge lies in deciding what to do and where to go next. With our high prices, it's not enough just to revise our insurance products and processes.

"We have to get beyond insurance, and become more intimately involved with our customers. If we're not feisty enough about grabbing new opportunities, everything we've worked for will quickly disappear."

But even as the restlessly ambitious Jorgenson set out to seize every fresh opportunity for radical growth, he found himself faced with a paradox that is peculiar to the business of health insurance.

The bigger you grow, the more income you generate, the more capital you need in reserve.

Why? To ensure you will be able to meet your obligations, pay all claims, and cover your legal solvency requirements. In IHI's case, that amounted to 32 million Danish Krone for every 100 million in earnings.

By 2000, IHI urgently needed an injection of capital to sustain its growth, and it was clear that the money wasn't going to come from the company's mutual insurance owners. Which is why, in November 2000, IHI was sold to a consortium of private equity funds called EQT.

While the deal provided IHI with a much-need launch pad for growth, it also led to a renewed bout of head-scratching and brainstorming within the organization. Where exactly was the growth going to come from? How far could you push the traditional boundaries of health insurance, without losing sight of the principles that build the business in the first place?

The challenge was monumental enough to match Jorgenson's vision: "I wanted to make IHI the most sought-after health insurance provider in the world."

As it turned out, the key to growth lay in a radical new understanding of the role of health insurance in the lives of corporate and individual customers.

Buy a health insurance policy, and what you're really buying is peace of mind: the knowledge that you'll be covered and protected in the event of illness or accident. But anyone with a working knowledge of medical matters will tell you there's a better way to invest your money. It's called prevention.

The concept of "wellness" – a proactive, holistic approach to the age-old goal of *mens sane in corpore sane* (a sound mind in a sound body) – began to take root at IHI, as a task team under the leadership of General Manager Ulrik Blinkenberg sought to define a new "market space" for the company.

"All our research was showing us that prevention and disease management are the best ways to cut down on the rising cost of healthcare," says Blinkenberg. "If people are encouraged to take active charge of their own health and well-being, it's a win-win for everybody – you, your family, your insurer and your employer."

Research also showed that more and more people were turning to the Internet for healthcare advice and information, and that growing numbers of consumers were prepared to spend money – their *own* money – on a wide range on alternative or complementary health treatments, such as massage, reflexology and homeopathic medicine.

For IHI, the market space had been defined. Traditional health insurance had its place, but the new style of customer was looking for something more: a pathway to a healthy, happy and productive life, inside and outside the workplace. The answer? Lifetime Health and Personal Safety Management.

Putting equal emphasis on each element of the equation, IHI crafted a mission statement that put the spotlight on new priorities and new opportunities for growth.

Among other things, staff committed themselves to being "indispensable to the quality of each customer's life", and helping to be "preventative and predictive about health and personal safety".

The grand ideal was a form of highly customized, individualized service that would truly distinguish IHI from its competitors. The key, Jorgenson knew, lay not just in the attitude and ability of IHI's people; it lay in the power of technology.

Not just the kind of technology that allowed you to process and settle a claim as swiftly as possible. That much had to be taken for granted. But imagine if you could use technology to supplement, complement and expand the traditional functions of healthcare itself.

An online doctor to answer your questions and assess your state of health. An online database of healthcare providers and country-specific medical and emergency information. A bank of educational material that could save your life, or at least help to improve your lifestyle. A personal health record. An RX translator for making sense of the scrawl on your prescription.

In short: technology that doesn't simply ensure that you get well; technology that helps you optimize your health.

Welcome to **Optimyse,**

IHI's personalized gateway to a better,

healthier way of life.

"Using interactive, Web-based technology," explains Ulrik Blinkenberg, "we're able to provide our customers with the kind of proactive information and advice they need to suit their own individual circumstances."

But Optimyse is only part of IHI's innovative approach to ensuring greater customer intimacy. The overall strategy is encapsulated in that simple definition of the new market space: Lifetime Health and Personal Safety Management.

"It's all about extending the boundaries of health insurance," adds Blinkenberg. "It's all about going beyond the industry norm."

In practice, that means a range of new products that include VIP policies for high net-worth individuals who want coverage for everything from alternative medicine to "aesthetic surgery"; incentive schemes that reward the user with reduced premiums or added cover; and a Health Consulting unit aimed at ensuring health and personal safety in the workplace.

Of course, all of this costs money, and the big challenge for IHI is to get its central message across to individuals and corporations: healthcare insurance doesn't have to be seen as a bottomless pit. It can – and should – be seen as an investment.

"An investment in the future," says Per Bay Jorgenson. "An investment in peace of mind. But more than anything else, an investment in a better, healthier way of living your life."

MY BLANK SLATE

Lessons learnt

Look to compete on greater value, not lower prices

Learn to turn a crisis into a global opportunity

Shorten the distance between the customer and the decision maker

Don't focus on "customers", focus on "the individual"

Think quick and make real-time decisions.
Leadership occurs at all levels

Keep staff motivated by allowing them to multi-task.
Let them see the complete picture all the time

Defy conventional wisdom. Every grudge purchase can be turned into real customer value

Find people who share your obsession for business

Effective communication begins with the ability to listen

Every opportunity is perishable. Grab it!

6

Wagging the dog

Taking on the world's biggest players from a garage

How Mark Shuttleworth **sold** his business, demonstrating the **epitome** of perfect timing

At the edge of the known universe, at the point on the map where knowledge and understanding give way to fear, conjecture and speculation, the mapmakers of old would inscribe a warning to those foolhardy enough to venture into uncharted territories.

"Hic sunt dracones," it would read. Here be dragons. Fire-breathing monsters with leathery wings, gaping jaws and flesh-tearing talons, they would lie in wait for ships that sailed too far and plunged off the end of the world, sending their crews screaming into the bottomless abyss. Today, of course, we know better.

There are no dragons. The world is round. All you need to navigate it is an up-to-date map, an eye for the distant horizon, and a vessel custom-built to transport your dreams to the shores of glorious reality. And yet, as the renowned social scientist and gestalt therapist Alfred Korzybski wrote in *Science and Sanity* in 1941, the map is not the territory.

Sometimes, even **when you think** you know where you are going, **fate** and the winds of change have a way of **steering** your ship on a very **different** course, usually at the **very last** minute.

Take Mark Shuttleworth, for example.

In 1995, he is a final-year student of Business Science at the University of Cape Town. Like many of his fellow students, he is an unashamed "party animal", enjoying an active social life on and off the campus. But unlike many, he has shied away from lining up a job for his first year in the real world, pinning his hopes instead on a scholarship that will allow him to devote his energies to the relative languor of post-graduate study.

It is not as if Shuttleworth, then only 21, is opposed to the notion of a hard day's work in return for a living wage. On the contrary, he has carved himself a lucrative niche as a freelance consultant to companies seeking to know more about a fledgling force for information, communication and – who knows? – maybe even commerce. The Internet.

Shuttleworth…
chasing dragons

So enthused and intrigued is Shuttleworth by the money-making possibilities of the medium, that he spends as many hours online as he does in argument with those faculty members who dispute his notion that the Internet has a role to play in the realm of business science.

It is, as he is frequently reminded, little more than a forum for inter-varsity communication, secondary research and mindless diversion, summed up by the unproductive, time-obliterating pursuit known as "surfing the web". But all this becomes academic on the day Shuttleworth learns he has failed in his bid to secure a post-graduate scholarship.

For the straight-A student, it is a blow to the ego that leaves him reeling. With nothing but burning ambition and a Bachelor of Business Science degree to his credit, he falls back on Plan B, forming a small consulting company whose very name suggests a radically different way of thinking. Thawte.

Operating from the garage of his parents' home in Durbanville, Cape Town, typically attired in shorts, sandals and T-shirt, Shuttleworth boldly sets sail for the jaws of waiting dragons.

His chosen terrain, borderless and seemingly boundless, is the terra incognita of the Internet, where vast fortunes may be reaped by those who can conquer the credit card bandits, the identity-thieves, the hackers and pirates of the high seas of electronic commerce.

The weapon for good in this war is a piece of binary code called a digital certificate, which acts as a passport or ID document for anyone seeking peace of mind in their dealings with online merchants. Through a protocol called SSL (Secure Sockets Layer), credit card numbers and other electronic data are scrambled and encrypted before transmission, allowing for easy authentication and rock-solid security of transaction.

Since fear of fraud has always been the single biggest obstacle to the growth of online commerce, digital certificates have become the most sought-after seals of approval and warrants of passage of the new age of business.

And it is here that Mark Shuttleworth, CEO and sole employee of Thawte Consulting, sets out to build a humble little business for himself.

Well, not so humble, and not so little. By the turn of the millennium only four years after his graduation from UCT Shuttleworth will have sold his company to his biggest rival, the American giant VeriSign, for $575 million. Famously, Shuttleworth will reward all 60 employees of Thawte (including two cleaners and a gardener) with $125,000 each, making them instant millionaires in their own currency. Some of these employees will become part of VeriSign. Others – bright, young and ambitious, party animals with a purpose – will join Shuttleworth in setting up a bold new business venture.

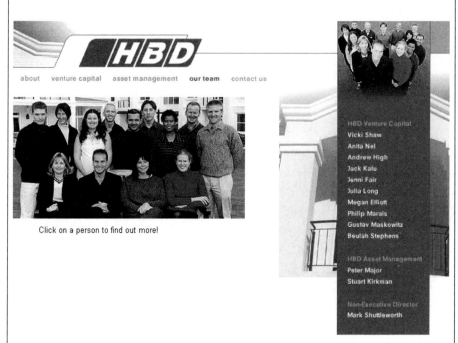

Click on a person to find out more!

HBD Venture Capital
Vicki Shaw
Anita Nel
Andrew High
Jack Kalu
Jenni Fair
Julia Long
Megan Elliott
Philip Marais
Gustav Maskowitz
Beulah Stephens

HBD Asset Management
Peter Major
Stuart Kirkman

Non-Executive Director
Mark Shuttleworth

Mark Shuttleworth and the HBD team…beyond Thawte

Grandly headquartered in Cape Town, with private landscaped gardens where staff are encouraged to "think quietly", an indoor pool, gym, library, unisex toilets and champagne always on ice to celebrate outstanding deals and achievements, the new company will manage assets and provide venture capital for fledgling entrepreneurs with big dreams and feasible ideas. The company will be called HBD. Which stands for: Here be Dragons.

The chief dragon-chaser himself will shift his base to London, running HBD and an education-oriented philanthropic foundation, TSF (The Shuttleworth Foundation), in-between the rigours of training for a much-coveted position as a civilian cosmonaut at Star City in Moscow. Eager to prove he is no ordinary "space tourist", Shuttleworth will conduct a series of onboard scientific experiments in conjunction with his alma mater, the University of Cape Town. Yes, there are new territories to be conquered, on earth and among the stars.

But the big question remains: how did Shuttleworth do it? He answers with a shrug and an impish smile.

"The usual suspects. Luck, timing, foolhardy bravery in the face of insurmountable odds, inspiration, perspiration, blood, sweat and tears."

Certainly, it is impossible to find fault with Shuttleworth's sense of timing. His deal with VeriSign went through just a few months before the company shed billions from its market value, as one of many victims of the meltdown in the global IT industry. As for luck, Shuttleworth has always been prepared to take the bad along with the good. What if he had won his post-graduate scholarship? What if he had lined up a steady, secure job with a large corporation?

"If life were totally predictable," he says, "it would be far less enjoyable.

"The temptation for a lot of success-driven people is to be miserable if they don't get what they want in every situation. I fight hard to get what I want – ask the people who have to work with me – but when things don't work out that way I accept there's a reason, and I start looking for the silver lining or the new opportunity."

But in the end, as Shuttleworth is quick to attest, it all comes down to three things. Blood, sweat, tears. With its vast resources and huge customer base in the USA, VeriSign may have appeared to exist in a realm beyond open challenge, particularly from a backyard operator at the opposite end of the planet.

But in a sphere of business where superiority of geographic location soon becomes irrelevant, Shuttleworth pushed the boundaries, and nudged the giant, through a combination of aggressive pricing and a focus on such lesser-served markets as Australia and Europe.

More than that, Shuttleworth outsmarted VeriSign and his other competitors with his innovative approach to digital certification, issuing single, encrypted certificates that allowed a company to register and certify all of its customers and employees at once.

The strategy paid off, over and over again. By 2000, Thawte owned 40 per cent of the global digital certification market, and was generating revenue of $90,000 a month, at prices that were two-thirds lower than VeriSign's. That's when the tail began wagging the dog. That's when VeriSign began making manoeuvres.

Still, Shuttleworth will be the first to admit that he still sometimes has second thoughts about Thawte.

"We could have been more aggressive in marketing some of our more industry-changing products," he says, citing cross-certification of companies as an example.

"We could have worked harder to sign up large ISPs as customers. And we could have created a higher priced product to compete at the high end of the market. I still don't understand pricing psychology. But the trick is to be happy with the way things work out, irrespective of the outcome."

"More important than

acknowledging
your mistakes,"

says Shuttleworth,

"is learning not to lose sleep over them."

It's all part of a business and personal philosophy that puts passion ahead of all other criteria for running with a project.

"Above all," he advises, "find a project you can be truly passionate about. That might mean refusing projects that have better financial prospects, or are more mainstream, or have less overt risk. The big mistake is to try to find the "Next Big Thing" based on what others are saying. By the time people are talking about it you are probably too far behind...you need to find the thing that resonates with yourself and your interests and your skills. And you need to build a strategy for success with the pieces you have at your disposal rather than the pieces you would like to have.

"Also, know what's really important to you, and make sure that you always stay true to that. The temptation to sacrifice everything to the pursuit of money or recognition is enormous and gets stronger the more successful you become. Remember that nobody ever died wishing they'd spent more time at the office. I'm always at the office, but then I'm also always in the playground. That's what's important to me."

Shuttleworth...turning venture capital from a
negative to a positive

What is also important to remember is that Shuttleworth pursued his own passion, and started his own enterprise, without the customary security of a large corporate sponsor or a tidy sum of venture capital. Looking back, he believes that the lack of venture funding was a negative that became a positive, inspiring him to work harder, faster and smarter in a fiercely competitive market.

But now that he is in a position to distribute venture capital himself, what are the qualities he looks for in other dragon chasers with other passions to pursue? He counts off the checklist.

"Insight into how the world is evolving. An understanding of what is important and what is irrelevant. A willingness to take the difficult path rather than the easy one if it means a better long-term position. Recognition of the fact that money can create as many problems for a start-up as it can solve. Clear insight into the fundamental forces at work within the marketplace. A plan to generate cash from operations, even if indirectly. And finally, a willingness to convince friends with high-paying steady jobs and good career prospects to join the venture *before* it raises finance!"

Today, having swapped his shorts, sandals and T-shirt for casual slacks, golf shirts and sensible shoes, Shuttleworth is upheld as a role-model of innovative entrepreneurship in action, even if he has faced criticism for relocating to London and indulging his boyhood fantasy of soaring into the cosmos.

But he shrugs off any tributes to his business acumen, insisting that he could use "a lot more discipline and training...for better or worse I've never been part of a large organization, and it shows."

Still, when it comes to confronting dragons, he is clearly a man who is able to overcome his own worst fears. Which doesn't mean he has an inordinate appetite for risk.

"I'm actually pretty risk averse by nature," he says. "I try to understand as many of the parameters as possible before taking a decision, which can make for painfully slow decision making and decisions that get reversed... sometimes repeatedly. I'm not very easy to work with.

"But the one thing I am totally fearless about is peer pressure. I'm absolutely willing to do something even if everybody else thinks it's a bad idea, if I'm confident that I have thought it through and can see a strategy for success. The strategy may fail, but if I think it's worth a shot I'll not ask permission or for anybody else's blessing.

"Half the fun is trying things that other people won't try. That doesn't mean jumping off a cliff to see what happens.

"It means being open to ideas that other people are not open to, simply because of their worldview."

From backyard garage to top of the world, from Cape Town to London to Outer Space, Mark Shuttleworth has managed to grasp the starry heights that others can only dream of.

But how, when you are not yet 30 and you are rich enough to spend $20 million on a ride into space, do you manage to retain the hunger that drove you to succeed and innovate in the first place?

"It's too early to say what I'm capable of doing in the future," says Shuttleworth. "I do find it much more difficult to pursue new ideas now, because I have so much less time to play with the Lego, so to speak. And so many more options...trying to find the space in which to focus is tough.

"What I'm trying to do is filter out all the things that are less interesting in favour of the ideas that genuinely pique my curiosity. The other thing I'm trying very hard to do is refuse to live inside the box other people create for me. In the eyes of many people I'm a 'business guy'.

"I'm not really. Nor am I a programmer, or a philanthropist, a technologist or even a networking guy. I'm me. All of those things, none of them, and some other pieces too. A whole mix of interests and ideas. And I hope to pursue each of those ideas, one by one, till my time is up."

"The result could be a

complete mess,

or a symphony,

but at least it will be my mess."

INNOVATION OPPORTUNITIES

Lessons learnt

Find a project you can be truly passionate about

Relish the bad luck as much as the good

Don't lose sleep over your mistakes

Don't be afraid to try things other people won't try

The Next Big Thing is always
something no-one is yet talking about

Timing is everything

Once you've made it,
find the courage to be yourself and have some fun

7

Harvesting ideas

The process of finding and funding radical innovation

How Deloitte Touche Tohmatsu's global approach to
harvesting ideas and fuelling
innovation is born out of the

limitless power of thought

Think. Think in the shower, think in the traffic, think when you're spinning up a hill on your cycle in the gym. Think when your mind is empty, think when it's weighed down with worry.

Think, because that's the way the world turns:

on the axis of an idea
whose time has come.

Let's see.

How about a proprietary system for assuring the safety and integrity of your biometric data? How about Michael Jordan's game jersey being tagged with a hologram right after the big game to eliminate fraud in the sports memorabilia industry? How about online, intelligent financial statements that automatically update financial analyst valuation models? How about selling, preparing and delivering professional services through virtual teams located all over the world?

We're at deloitteinnovation.com, an online forum for the sharing and airing of ideas that are wild or outrageous or – every now and again – so sensible and practical that you wonder why nobody thought of them before.

**Deloitte
Touche
Tohmatsu**

About Us

Services

Industries

Locations

Careers

Publications

What's New

Site Search

Feedback

Welcome to
Deloitte Touche Tohmatsu

Wherever you are in the world, we'll make your business count.

The national practices of Deloitte Touche Tohmatsu are dedicated to delivering world-class service to our world-class clients in more than 130 countries.

Our mission is to help our clients and our people excel. These two forces come together in a powerful combination of wide-ranging services in every major business center in the world.

Our services include assurance and advisory, management consulting, and tax advice to hundreds of the world's biggest and most respected companies, including the world's largest manufacturer, 5 of the 25 largest banks and four of the largest trading companies.

Our people also listen in over 100 languages; beyond the major economies many of our professionals serve and assist the emerging markets, advising governments and institutions throughout Central Europe and Asia Pacific.

Globalization, changing societal priorities, and access to real-time information are fundamentally changing the way organizations do business. We help our clients meet the challenge of demonstrating globally responsible business practices while balancing social, environmental, and financial performance.

To find out more about what Deloitte Touche Tohmatsu can do for you, explore our Web site.

**Which Big Five Firm is running
rings around its competition?**

the answer is
**Deloitte
Touche
Tohmatsu**

Deloitte Touche Tohmatsu's online portal, gateway to
a web of services that encircle the world

The point is, somebody probably has, just as somebody once thought of trapping electricity in the filaments of a glass bulb, or squeezing waves of sound down a length of cable, or transmitting text and images through fine strands of fibre at 4320 terabits a second.

Every idea, no matter how fanciful, no matter how lucid, begins as a chain of thought floating freely through the ether.

The challenge is to bring it down to earth, tether it to a business plan and a funding model, and release it into the wild to see how fast and how far it travels before it takes root.

But first: you have to chase the Big Idea. You have to set individual and collective imaginations on fire, stir the juices of creative thinking, clear a space for the planting, nurturing and harvesting of the small seeds of possibility that dwell within the heart of every global enterprise.

Let's take Deloitte Touche Tohmatsu, for example. Here we have a global professional services firm that employs close to 90,000 people in over 135 countries (732 cities), and serving nearly one-fifth of the world's largest companies with turnovers and/or assets in excess of $1 billion each, among its clients.

Chances are you've heard of Deloitte, as it's commonly known around the world. Chances are, if someone asked you to define the firm's spread of services, that your answer would be: auditing, accounting and tax services.

After all, this is the firm started by William Welch Deloitte, the 19th-Century adventurer turned accountant, and George Touch, the Scottish auditor who added an e to the end of his name because he was tired of correcting Englishmen who didn't know that it was supposed to rhyme with "loch". But the thing is, in the space of a hundred years, a lot more than a name can change.

Today, Deloitte Touche Tohmatsu – that's Admiral Nobuzo Tohmatsu, the Japanese naval attaché who became a public accountant at the age of 57, and went on to head up the firm that would eventually find a global partner big enough to match its own ambitions – is still in the tax and auditing business.

But when you're that close to a company's business, you begin to get a sense of the prospects and possibilities that lie beyond the bottom line.

So today, under the broad umbrella of "professional services", Deloitte is also recognized as a global leader in such diverse areas as legal services, human capital consulting, wealth management for private clients, IT systems integration and forensic investigations. But for a firm as big as Deloitte, as ambitious as Deloitte, as resourceful as Deloitte...even all of that isn't enough in its pursuit to be the top professional services firm.

Which is why, at the start of a new millennium, the firm commits itself to growing its global business beyond every target, beyond every expectation. How? By radically changing the way it sees itself, the way it does business. By thinking different, by thinking big. And more than anything else, by creating a culture and a climate for innovation to flourish at every level of the organization.

To kick-start the process, Deloitte establishes the Service Innovation Board (SIB), a global springboard for generating big business through the generation of big ideas.

The SIB is entrusted with a dual mission: to grow the firm's existing businesses and service lines, and to pursue, champion and swiftly shepherd innovative new ideas and opportunities through the organization's complex structure.

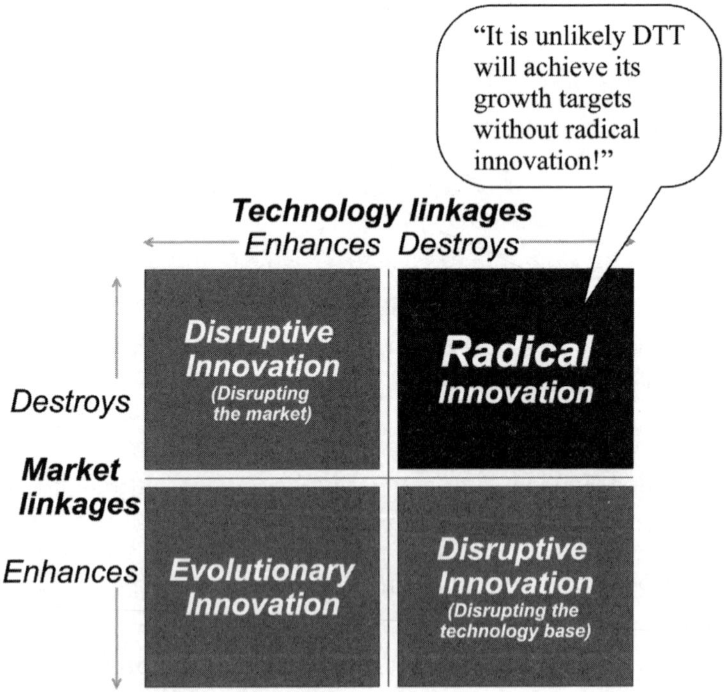
"It is unlikely DTT will achieve its growth targets without radical innovation!"
Technology linkages
Enhances
Destroys
Market linkages
Destroys
Enhances
Disruptive Innovation (Disrupting the market)
Radical Innovation
Evolutionary Innovation
Disruptive Innovation (Disrupting the technology base)

"We committed the firm to achieving huge growth targets, in some economies that were barely even growing," recalls Jean-Paul Picard, Chairman of the SIB.

Driven by these radical targets, Deloitte took an "intellectual decision" to expand into areas that often had little direct linkage to the firm's existing business.

In other words,

Jean-Paul Picard

the firm **committed** itself to **creating something out of a void.** Determined to step into **the risky world of radical innovation,** Deloitte knew that **evolutionary change alone** would not be enough.

But beyond that murky, swirling void, the firm's vision of the future was crystal-clear. Deloitte wanted to be the best and fastest-growing professional services firm in the world. In 1998, in the Big Five of firms that dominate the industry – PricewaterhouseCoopers, KPMG, Ernst & Young and Andersen being the others – DTT held position Number Four. To get

Radical innovation is
critical to achieving DTT's
growth strategy

Welcome to the Zone...setting out to turn dreams into reality

closer to the top, the firm would have to grow by leaps and bounds. The traditional growth target of around 15 per cent suddenly seemed too modest for comfort.

"Our goal was simple," adds Picard. "We wanted to achieve an average annual growth rate of more than 22 per cent. Our immediate goal was to leapfrog the others in the Big Five, to move from the number four spot to number two overall."

With the Service Innovation Board acting as a catalyst, Deloitte set out to grow its existing business around the world, and to identify and incubate a series of new service lines.

Clearly, that kind of growth would not be achieved by simply expanding the current business. Whether by organic means or through strategic mergers and acquisitions, new clients would have to be found, new offerings developed, new industries explored. DTT was going to have to get bigger and better in a hurry. In the words of the firm's global CEO, James E. Copeland Jr: "I'd rather be big and quick than small and quick!"

There was only one way DTT would be able to live up to its radical vision of the future. *Innovate.* Innovate bigger, innovate better, innovate quicker. To make it happen, the firm was going to have to build a place where ideas themselves could be incubated, nurtured, given shape and form. Not a building of bricks and mortar – Deloitte Touche Tohmatsu already has enough of those.

This would be a space rather than a place, a forum where fleeting thoughts could be herded, exposed to heat and light, and – assuming they passed the test – transformed into something approaching solid matter.

This would be... The Innovation Zone.

But before we step into the Zone, let's pose a question or two: what exactly does innovation have to do with a firm like Deloitte Touche Tohmatsu?

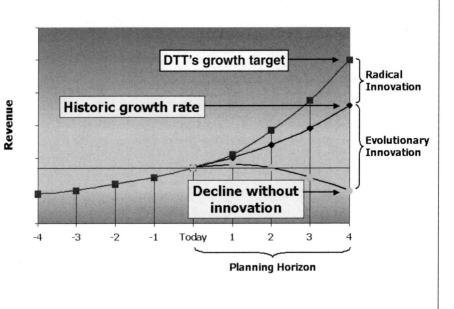

How can you realistically expect and encourage a large, successful, established hierarchical business to become passionate about generating ideas and re-inventing itself?

After all, here was a firm that was already in the Big League. Already doing fine. Already growing its business. But complacency is the enemy of innovation, and Deloitte, spurred by the onset of a new and exciting century, had already decided that "good enough" wasn't good enough.

The intellectual decision had been taken. The targets had been set. All that remained, was to make the future happen.

Across the world of Deloitte, innovators sprang into action; ideas began taking the fast route to reality.

A team of "Innovation Activists" led by Louis Geeringh, Global Executive Director of the SIB, was asked to start the ball rolling.

"We were working under very tight time-constraints," recalls Geeringh. "We realized we wouldn't get the new ideas to come from our people if we sat back and waited for our innovation systems and processes to be fully developed."

Geeringh and fellow innovators

The immediate priority for Deloitte was to grow its existing businesses and service lines, particularly in countries where the firm was "under-scaled" in comparison with market demand.

Then Deloitte began shifting its focus to the future. "We began by taking a good look at the businesses we were in," says Geeringh, "and more importantly, the businesses we weren't."

In days gone by, such market and business opportunities may have been subjected to intensive market research and internal and external feasibility analysis. But now, the attitude was: jump right in and get going.

"We deployed a small team of people from very diverse backgrounds and competencies," says Picard.

"People in corporate finance, strategy, economics and project management. People who thrive on the challenge of business building and the ability to do so without a manual."

Deloitte had already committed itself to creating something out of the void. The void, of course, is where all ideas are born, and here the void would be given form and substance through a forum that existed in the ether.

The Innovation Zone is a public-domain website (www.deloitteinnovation.com), accessible to anyone with a deloitte in their e-mail address.

"The Innovation Zone," explains Geeringh, "is a key part of our strategy to grow the business beyond its historical, scientifically backed-up projections, by allowing anyone who has a stake in that growth to participate in the free generation of new business ideas."

More than a think tank, more than a suggestion box, the Innovation Zone is the bedrock of the future, and the future, as everyone knows, begins with the click of a mouse on a button marked SUBMIT.

Whatever your position in the organization, wherever in the world you may be, you log-in, submit your proposal – a few lines, a few hundred words, with the system helping you structure the outline of a business plan – and you sit back and wait for the gears to turn.

A comprehensive approach to finding and funding innovation

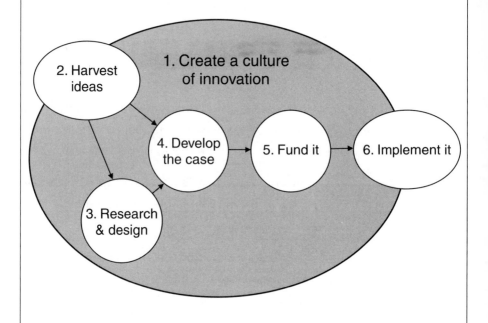

"Every idea goes into a database," says Picard, "and the interactive system forces it to fly through the internal processes. There's no logjam created by the hierarchy."

Every idea is judged according to a universal scoring system, on the basis of its overall feasibility and viability. If it fails, it stays on the database, because even the wildest of ideas might turn out to have merit or relevance further down the line. If it passes, it goes onto the next stage. The interview.

Here, an internal panel will quiz the progenitor or progenitors of the proposal, seeking to explore the deeper thinking behind it, and analyze any other ideas that have spun off or developed from the original free-floating thought. The next step: maturity.

The idea is championed, supported, protected from the "corporate antibodies" that rally by reflex against anything that looks too different or looks like it might cost too much money.

During this phase, Deloitte's "intrapreneurs" will be allocated resources to develop their idea, buy research reports, and "work the network" of other intrapreneurs, leaders and idea-mongers.

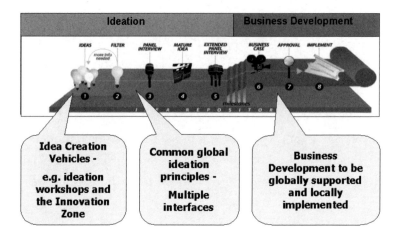

Many will have been through workshops, or will have participated in the development of an idea. Should the idea be felt to have "significant" merit and potential, it will be herded to maturity with the help of full-time staff from the SIB. And what about ideas that fail to make the grade?

As John Kutz, SIB Ideation Process Leader explains, they're not simply discarded by the wayside. "Ideas that are not matured through the SIB are channelled to the right home in Deloitte for consideration, with the contributor or contributors being kept in the loop on developments."

Geeringh: "It's about the right people, with the right idea, at the right time."

Often, an idea will be submitted by more than one contributor, with the same basic concept being explored from several different angles. Deloitte makes the most of this diversity of creative thought and action, by allowing contributors to collaborate in small groups or "groves", where even the roughest idea can be fine-tuned and groomed for the big time.

Once an idea becomes a matured value proposition, it is submitted to further scrutiny by an extended panel, made up of Deloitte staff, outside experts and possibly even clients. Beyond this stage, says Picard, it's not an idea anymore. It's a business in germination. What will it need to grow? Hard work. Research. Passion. And money.

If it makes it – because this is business, not philanthropy – what's in it for the author of the idea? Glory, self-esteem, recognition. And money.

"On a monthly basis," says Geeringh, "we'll reward the person who contributed the best idea with a bonus of $2000 or more. But if it's a great idea that allows us to start generating serious profit, there's no limit to what we'll pay out.

"No limit at all.
Our global leaders are committed
to paying hundreds of thousands of
dollars for successful new businesses."

Naturally, such ideas are few and far between. As soon as you create an open forum for new business opportunities, particularly with such a handsome incentive at its core, you're going to find yourself dealing with an unusually high ratio of noise to signal.

But as Picard admits: "Even a bad idea can turn out to be a not-so-bad idea when you start applying some thought to it. Our problem is that we simply don't have enough bandwidth for the volume of ideas that come in. The real value of the process lies in the business development side. And that's where our pipeline is limited and where our core focus is."

Think. Think Deloitte. Think business.
Think big.

How about a service to translate complex financial statements from one language to another whilst recognising differences in accounting standards?

How about a smart new system – call it ShareTrust – that allows company secretaries to tame the complexities of managing global stock options for employees?

How about a specialist Environmental Consulting service, aimed at helping companies fulfil their corporate governance responsibilities, while generating income from such key areas as carbon trading?

How about a *real* value-added service, for analyzing, interpreting and converting vast chunks of corporate data?

There you have just a few ideas that made it through the process. Ideas that made – and are making – money for Deloitte. But as much as the process is internally driven, as much as it seeks to encourage and reward innovation within the organization, the Zone, by definition, must be broad enough to embrace anyone who claims ownership of an idea whose time has come.

"There are millions of incredible products, millions of incredible pieces of software, just sitting in closets around the world," says Louis Geeringh. "We'll never know about them, because they'll never be exposed to the light.

"No matter how good it is, an idea means nothing unless it can be developed and applied commercially."

So when a young entrepreneur approaches Deloitte with what he insists is "a really outstanding idea" – an e-commerce-based dispute resolution service – the company doesn't show him the door.

Well, they do, except it's the door of an office, with a desk and a PC, where he will be free to sit for three weeks, fine-tune his idea, with the entire global Deloitte network at his disposal, and then come into an interview and convince a panel that the seed of a business is ready to be nurtured. Just add money.

Setting up the internal venture capital fund	Managing the fund
Create an investment mandate. In addition to usual issues, such as, maximum investment size, industry split, etc, the mandate includes the following: • Preferred valuation method • Reporting methods (both within the fund and within the investments) • Method for assessing the size of the return to match the risk • Develop a complete reporting structure that is in full compliance with the lastest global standards • Appoint and train fund managers • Appoint and train business mentors • Train directors and committee members • Develop governance structures for the fund that will allow the risks to be managed in an orderly fashion	Identify the tools required to administer the fund: • Tool to harvest and screen innovation from across the business – something equivalent to Innovation Zone • Workflow management tool to the fund's specific requirements • Perform detailed pre-investment screening • Perform due diligence work • Investment management • Diagnostic services, for distressed investments and investment exits • Identify which of the above should be sourced externally

Which raises the next big, tough question. Just how does a large organization manage the funds allocated for radical innovation?

Shareholders who demand the best returns every quarter will almost certainly not want to see a successful business "squandering" hard earned cash on radical projects with dubious prospects.

Managing funds allocated for innovation inside an organization, is becoming as vital and arduous a task as the venture capital business has become in the open marketplace. Many large organizations have chosen to outsource this responsibility, and this in turn has become a substantial business opportunity for Deloitte.

But whether you outsource or create an internal corporate venture fund to manage investments in radical innovation, the principles and guidelines remain the same.

The management and governance of a venture capital fund needs to be clearly defined to ensure that it becomes a well-governed business, generates good returns and achieves strategic economic objectives with the lowest risk to its stakeholders.

Deloitte has made radical innovation an integral part of its corporate DNA, and the firm is now encouraging clients to take the same radical medicine. Customized versions of *Innovation Zone* are being rolled out to clients, creating resonance with the marketplace.

The idea. The people.

The feasibility.
If each component passes the test,

it's green for go, green for # money.

Think. Think radical. Think big. Think beyond traditional boundaries and perceptions. Because innovation can come from anywhere.

"Perhaps it's counter-intuitive," says Geeringh, "but much innovation seems to occur at the edge of the empire – in our case in countries such as Hong Kong, Greece, South Africa and Australia. When all the odds are against you and you have to do things out of necessity to stay in business, it breeds a certain type of hunger in people – and essential nutrients to make radical innovation flourish."

Here's the bottom line.

Knowledge + Action = Power

It's not just about money. It's not just about profit. It's about the right people, with the right idea, at the right time. Get that formula right, and you're in business.

MY INNOVATION ZONE

Lessons learnt

Radical business growth can be achieved through
setting out-of-the-box "unachievable" targets

Given the chance, people come up with
a flood of dynamic ideas

Speed of response in assessing and evaluating
proposals is key

The right tools make innovation manageable and pervasive

Identify the "low hanging fruit" opportunities,
and develop those first

Internal "venture capital funds" and "investment banks" are
a vital part of the implementation of innovation in large
organizations

Innovation must be driven outside of
day-to-day business processes

New ventures need to be assessed according to new rules,
and nurtured outside the normal business culture

Think beyond traditional boundaries and perceptions –
innovation often comes from "the edge of the empire"

8

Herding cats

The golden thread that runs through radical innovation

How to attract and retain
the brightest young things,
and the implications of working with them

If you're a fan of cowboy movies – and be honest now, who isn't? – you'll probably have fond memories of an old epic called *Red River*, starring John Wayne and his younger sidekick, Montgomery Clift.

It's about the battle for land, the battle between generations, the battle between the pioneers of the untamed West, and the indigenous tribes who already occupied the territory. But mostly, it's about cattle.

The centrepiece of the story is a long, gruelling trek to drive a herd of more than 6000 steers northwards across the raging river of the title, and on towards Kansas. There are thunderstorms, sandstorms, gunfights, fistfights, stampedes.

Even if you aren't a fan of cowboy movies, it's a film worth watching, because it seems to say something about the relentless determination, grim resolve, and inexhaustible energy required to get almost any big project on the road. This applies particularly in the world of business.

Substitute budgets for sandstorms, competitors for fistfights, and stock-market listings for stampedes, and you begin to get the picture.

In the preceding chapters of this book, our case studies of radical innovation are characterized by individuals actively driving their organizations away from traditional industrial-age management – the days of managing people as if we were herding cattle.

First, we'd put each of the vertical smokestack organizations, like administration, marketing and sales, into a different pen. As an employee, you'd be fenced off and actively encouraged not to jump the fence. If you did so, without permission, then you could expect to be punished. The rules were well understood.

The concept that 'Work is what you do, not where you go' had not yet surfaced.

It was a world of 9 to 5. You had to be there, in your pen, to be considered to be of value. Every now and then you would see a cowboy on a large horse ride into the adjacent pen and start whipping the cattle into shape.

"Gee, I wonder what they did wrong," you would think to yourself. The group in your pen would immediately decide to keep a low profile and do as they were told, lest they too be subjected to such punishment. You never questioned your superiors. After all, they knew best.

But that was the old world. Things have changed.

Today staff are actively encouraged to challenge all the hoary old rules. To think independently, and listen to the market.

Sometimes, it seems as if business in an innovative world has become pure anarchy.

In spite of our opening contention that there is no golden bullet for radical innovation, it must have emerged in your subconscious that there is a very strong golden thread running through our stories of radical innovation.

Managing People Is Like Herding Cats

by Warren Bennis

Herding Cats Across the Supply Chain

by Ram Reddy

Herding Cats – Multiparty Mediation in a Complex World

edited by Chester A. Crocker

This golden thread is one of unreasonable, restless people, for whom the best is never good enough, for whom there is always a better way. To them there are no imperatives, no rigidly-defined boundaries, no "cattle pens". There are always other ways of seeing the problem. To them, there are opportunities in every business black hole.

These are the people who thrive despite the environment. They capitalize on everything around them, good or bad. They have access to exactly the same resources as others, yet they always seem able to create more value.

They are exactly the kind of people that many good managers hate to have working for them! In fact, it's often said they can't be "managed".

If managing a business was like "herding cattle", then this is the equivalent of "herding cats".

The phrase has come into common usage in high-technology circles to describe the difficulty of managing the seemingly unmanageable. Just look at the titles of some recent business books and articles opposite.

Yes, everyone's talking about the challenge of herding cats. And at the heart of the dilemma, we find a classic Generation Gap: most of the "herders" will be people in their 40s and 50s, while most of the "cats" will be twentysomethings. It's the Baby Boomers versus the Generation Xers. Different points of view, different sets of values.

As a "Baby Boomer" of the Woodstock generation, you will probably find little difficulty managing other Boomers: "Anything's possible. Let's get out there and do it!" You may even have become resigned to the fixation on security and loyalty so characteristic of your parents' generation – the so-called Silent Generation. But now, the bright young people you are trying to attract into business are just not playing the game. They don't seem to play by the same rules, they don't have the same values. And yet, you are completely dependent on their energy, drive and technical skills.

All the more so in an organization driven by the radical innovation imperative.

Aletha Ling, one of the young veterans of the rollercoaster dot com world, is a person who knows a bit about these young "cats", and the difficulty of creating an organization around them.

In 1995, Ling, together with Anne Czerner, created waves in the South African computer industry by leaving her job as Software Executive at IBM and starting a highly successful software solutions business, Software Futures.

Software Futures quickly captured the imagination of the market. Within just three years, the company reached a market cap of more than R100 million. Naturally, with the insatiable demands for cash inherent in high-growth companies, it became the target of an increasingly acquisitive market. It was acquired by CCH in a classical cash plus shares deal where the shares dominated. The innovative Software Futures was now part of a much bigger entity. Different priorities, different cultures, different principles.

Without knowing it,

Ling had stepped into quicksand.

Shortly after Ling's company was merged into them, the CCH group spiralled downwards on the back of poor publicity and worse press coverage. Ling was appointed Group CEO in an attempt to pull the company out of its dive. At this stage it seems there was nothing that could come between CCH and the inevitable. At a late stage, with the share price at just 5 per cent of its peak just two years before, Ling led the acquisition of the company by MGX.

In a heady period of less than three years, Ling's fortunes had fluctuated wildly. She had experienced the leadership equivalent of a journey to hell and back. Who said radical innovation was easy?

She reflects: "We built Software Futures around three key tenets: Radical Innovation, Breakthrough Implementation and Thought Leadership. We believed these would translate into serious value for our clients, but we knew they would have to be built on a very different business model and with very different people.

"Our industry – information technology – has changed a lot. It's fundamentally about very talented people, professionals who don't suffer fools gladly, and who have great freedom of choice when it comes to deciding who they want to work for. Being a leader in such an organization requires a very different mindset from that of ten years ago.

Ling: A life on the rollercoaster

"To create the environment for growth and innovation we created something called the 'spinout model', and what it entailed was creating a leadership environment that would make room for a new, younger breed of individual.

"The spinout model was devised to encourage entrepreneurship by allowing ideas to surface, and then giving free rein to the individual with the passion and ability to turn the idea into a successful venture. This is the 'white space' required for radical innovation. It was in fact an early form of what venture capitalists came to call the incubator model, except that it was run inside the company.

Lessons from the rollercoaster

When there is less hierarchy of management,
and more philosophy of leadership,
a great deal of trust becomes necessary

Open comunication builds
organizational robustness against outside forces

The more appropriate the culture, the more the
dream is shared, the more likely it is that individuals
will make good decisions

While talented young professionals are
typically self-directing, with great skills,
motivation and drive, they still need to work within a team

Build companies that can survive in any kind of market –
not just bull markets

Leaders provide the "energy" that
drives an organization

Leaders must motivate and enthuse,
not by exacting obedience
but by inspiring great performance

It's easy to succeed in
predictable markets.
In turbulent times, innovation becomes the key
to sustained growth

"The great thing about this approach is that it allows individuals to think about and conceptualize new ideas, but it also meant that they have to take ownership and responsibility for turning the idea into a real business venture. This, for me, is the difference between dreamers and entrepreneurs. People have to accept real ownership. The declining fortunes of CCH had a real impact on many people. It significantly changed the environment in which Software Futures operated."

Ling: the joy of herding cats

What are the lessons Aletha Ling has learnt from her rollercoaster experience? Take a look at the summary opposite.

"Get this right,"
she says of what she has learnt,
"and herding cats becomes
a pleasure and a joy,
rather than a chore."

Would she do it all again? As a serial innovator, Aletha Ling probably knows no other way. Today, as Strategy Executive of MGX, Ling is taking great pleasure in innovating and helping her new company grow into the future.

During the last decade of the 20th Century, the model of conspicuous success and an attractive icon for the "cats" has undoubtedly been the Microsoft Corporation.

Today, in an internal meeting at the Redmond campus, the hulk of Steve Ballmer, CEO of Microsoft, cuts a mean figure as he stands at the head of a crowded table. Just as Bill Gates has been the "mind" of Microsoft, so has Ballmer become its passionate "heart". Sometimes blunt and aggressive, he gesticulates wildly, hands and arms in constant motion:

"Burn this into your brain... LOVE CUSTOMERS!"

It's interesting that a company as successful as Microsoft has only recently begun to actively embrace the customer. Previously the focus on product excellence and the execution of ever more complex projects was what attracted "the cats" into its orbit. In fact, for much of the past decade, Microsoft has been the magnet for bright young things, and that has undoubtedly been one of the reasons for the company's success. Many companies have tried to replicate that success, but the formula has proved to be based just as much on the power of products such as Windows and Office, as on Bill Gates' freewheeling approach.

As a youngster, Gates was the archetypal non-conformist. A university drop-out, proud of the fact that his office contained no management books, he felt "smart enough" without formal training. He exhorted his staff to follow his example.

"Why do we need an executive training function – it's all common sense!"

he would say.

Microsoft's share-option culture was built around his determination for employees to "feel the pain and share the gain". He believed every individual action would have an effect on the share price. He encouraged outrageous performance. On a rating of 1 to 5, achievement of all targets would only get you as far as a 3. And that was simply not acceptable for any Microsoft "cat"!

Terry Annecke, a long-serving Microsoft marketing executive, remembers how the company's recruitment strategy was built in Gates' image. "What we wanted were 'smarts' – self-starters driven by challenge, who could not only inspire but manage themselves. If it wasn't for national labour legislation I'm not sure that we would have had employment contracts. We measured people totally on outputs. The aspects measured were wrapped up in the acronym SMART – objectives must be Specific, Measurable, Achievable, Results-oriented and Time specific. Measures that individuals could relate to – they had to set their own goals and agree them with their team leaders. The reason the word 'achievable' was in there was that they typically set completely unachievable goals for themselves!"

Today, many of the original Microsoft millionaires no longer work for the company, but most of the billionaires still do. One of those is Steve Ballmer, who took over the operational reigns of the business when Gates made himself Chief Software Architect. Today Gates oversees a massive R&D budget of more than $4 billion, much of it in primary research with no known outcomes. This is the stuff that many cats dream of.

The demonstrative Steve is full of
passionate advice for his people:
"Be straightforward. Get rid of barriers.
Get it done.
If you think something is wrong,
say so quickly. Get help."
Each element punctuated by a punch in the air.
The cats love it. They love Steve.

He attracts top cats to Microsoft with monotonous regularity. He attracted Bob Herbold from Procter & Gamble, to become Microsoft's COO and their first silver-haired cat, a 50-plus-year-old with the mind of a Generation Xer. Then came the coup of Rick Belluzzo. The softly spoken outsider, who was named COO within 18 months of joining the company.

Belluzzo, former number two at HP and former CEO of Silicon Graphics, has morphed into Microsoft-speak with the greatest of ease. He frequently talks of an era of "technology schizophrenia" where the same person takes on a different profile and personality with every device and application he uses.

As the UK's *Guardian* newspaper puts it: "Belluzzo provides a marked contrast to the company's uncharismatic founder, Bill Gates – or his ebullient, bullet-headed number two, Steve Ballmer. The three act as the Good, the Bad and the Ugly – with Belluzzo acting as the junior foil to Bill the Bully and a chief executive who looks like Uncle Fester."

Steve, the Good Cat, is one of the few Harvard grads in Microsoft, and he has taken it upon himself to make the company more customer focused. The original distribution model that created massive organizations out of their distributors and dealers is being expanded to embrace the customer.

He admits that ten years ago the Microsoft culture was so "way out", that it was easy to attract the cats. Today the competition for their hearts and minds is far tougher. Today campus graduates have so much more choice and are aware of the power their skills and attitudes wield. So many of the cats now have their own radical catteries! Today Microsoft has to focus more strongly on creating the environment that allows cats to flourish – more than just share options, more than great products and great projects.

In the race to win the hearts of the bright young things, the systems environment at Microsoft has been turned into something of a competitive advantage. All administrative systems are integrated into an approach based on the need to survive in business without a secretary or administrative assistants.

Microsoft has one of the highest administrator to cat ratios in the world, close to 1:25.

Any function from travel booking to skills development can be performed directly online by the cats themselves. Want to order a PC? No need for an executive cat to give the job to an administrator. Everything from choice, configuration and approval is online. Order and delivery is available through a joint venture with Compaq. Payment, delivery and installation follows seamlessly. The complete value network is integrated, so that the hassles are taken away from the cats. They only do what they love – or at least that's the idea!

Some lessons? Cats want to be a part of a successful company, share in the development of successful products, and enjoy the opportunity to make them even better. No project, no deadline, no matter how daunting, is impossible. Cats don't get put off by the scale of the problem.

Take Brian Valentine. Master communicator, master motivator, flamboyant trouble-shooter and process manager behind the momentous success of Windows 2000, one of the most solid operating systems ever built – and built almost on time! Valentine strolled into Microsoft as a cat 13 years ago, and stayed that way. At the height of pressure to deliver Windows 2000, he walked the hallways at Redmond decked out in a T-shirt that proclaimed "I yell because I care!"

When you herd cats
you can't pussyfoot around.
Don't try the usual office politics.
The cats want you to be open and honest.

Deal with pain
quickly.

"I was just the cheerleader who helped the team get across the finish line," says Valentine. If you're herding cats, you need cheerleaders to craft direction out of the totally desirable chaos.

But it's one thing to herd cats and strive for innovation in a company that stands at the forefront of the IT revolution.

It's quite another when you're running an organization whose main line of business just happens to be

herding cattle.
Or at least, herding cars, trucks, boats, planes, trains, freight and commuters.

How do you innovate, how do you herd cats, when you're running Transnet, the biggest parastatal on the African continent?

Let's talk to Mafika Mkwanazi, managing director of Transnet. Here we have a company where authority is cautiously delegated, and where the consequences of failure can result in powerful public censure. Even so, Mkwanazi recognizes the need to provide "white space" for people to explore.

Transnet MD
Mkwanazi

"As a small boy I would lug heavy boxes of peanuts and handkerchiefs to sell to train passengers on the Faraday line between Soweto and Johannesburg."

Back at home, Mafika, the youngest of four children, would light a candle at night, then read and study into the early hours, an effort that kept him in the top five in his school.

"I will never forget where I came from. Yes, there was poverty, but my mother gave me the greatest gift – the space and support to do whatever I wanted to do."

He is now applying that thinking to the future of Transnet, breaking up the unwieldy conglomerate into smaller focused business entities with private sector involvement in each one. "In five years I want to see just ten people in Transnet head office, just a core of people managing the investments and leaving the businesses to focus on what they do best. This transition will not be easy, we will need to bridge the generational and ideological divide. We must give more space to the operating companies, allow them to be viable and thrive."

But a South African reality is that most of our young people will not find jobs in the corporate world. Mafika himself has a teenaged son and daughter. What would his advice be to them?

"I would encourage them to see themselves as global workers, to develop the specific skills that are valued globally and to get into that growing job market."

True to his word, he has involved Transnet in training youngsters to capitalize on the global market, for example by funding a maritime training institute, which will help develop skills that are in short supply worldwide. "We have to focus our innovations at the vast global market."

What Mafika's mother intuitively gave to **her youngest child is what every corporation ought** to give to their people –

the space to flourish.

Think about it, would you really build a successful sports team by getting each of your star players to conform? Wouldn't you want each of them to exercise their own particular skill to the utmost? To push the barriers! See how far they can take it!

Similarly, we should not shape our cats to the corporate mould. We should allow each and every one to exercise their unique skills, and let the market be the judge of the value they add.

It takes bold leadership and the courage to allow for risk and failure. To allow for constant criticism of the status quo. To thrive in the uncomfortable environment created by never-satisfied cats. Creating this environment will attract the bright young things, and make the difference between success and failure.

Innovation thrives on open leadership that lives on the edge of chaos and finds inspiration in uncertainty. That's why managing innovation is like herding cats.

If it's so tough why even start attracting cats to your business?

Why do it at all?

EDS, the global IT services firm, ran a wonderful advertising campaign that captured the essence of this idea.

To me, the most powerful concept is in the closing line in the 30-second ad:

"When you bring a herd into town,

there ain't a feeling like it
in the world!"

Herding cats is not just about the challenges of "herding" or leading highly talented professionals. Herding cats is ultimately about the rewards – about the pride and satisfaction you feel when you bring the herd into town.

MY RADICAL TO-DO LIST

Lessons learnt

Thrive on chaos and uncertainty, it's the new way of the world

Get ready to have the cats question
every aspect of your business

Capitalize on the diversity of generations

Replace the hierarchy of management,
with a philosophy of leadership

Create an open corporate environment
in which entrepreneurs can thrive

Spin out radical new ventures to create a white space culture

Learn from those who win
and those who step into the quicksand

Understand that cats don't get put off
by the scale of the problem

When you herd cats you can't pussyfoot around
– be open, honest and quick

Get ready to herd cats,
there's no feeling like it in the world!

9

Strategic Thinking and Strategic Action™

A process to make your radical future a matter of choice

Ideally, what do you want your business to be?

How do you turn bright ideas into commercial realities?

How can you choose your business and personal future?

This chapter will introduce you to a process that will help you move from inside-out thinking about your business, to outside-in thinking about your business.

I'll show you how to stop asking "What is my business?" and focus on "What do I want my business to be?"

But before we get onto that, what did you think of the stories of our radical innovators? Inspirational stuff? Scary? Invigorating?

Right now you're probably thinking:

"That's all very well,

but
how do I start?"

Before we commence our journey into radical innovation, before we pass "Go", let's look at what, in my mind, remains the key prerequisite to radical innovation. At a macro level, we can start with a kind of "trick" question, the answer to which will forever determine how innovative your business can be. So, be careful how you answer.

This is the question:

"What is your business?"

Easy isn't it? But think again. What is your value proposition to the marketplace? Not your perception, but your customers' perception. Whatever customers value, they will pay for in direct proportion to the perceived value. Goodness. And, that translates into long-term profits. Don't interpret their "value" statement as what you *wish* it was.

Ask the market.
Ask your customers.
What do your customers
perceive value to be?
Listen carefully to the response.

Believe it! Act on it!

What is Black and Decker's business? Power tools? Electric drills?

As a non-technical customer I know that their real value proposition to me is simple – it's just "holes". Their ads have consistently left me feeling technically challenged. Why do I need to know the number of revolutions per minute of an electric motor when all I need is a "hole".

You see, I would suggest that, like me, many customers only see the drill, the drill bits, the extension cords and the associated paraphernalia as an unnecessary hurdle to achieving "the hole".

I would suggest to you that from many customers' point of view, their business is just "holes".

Think about the organization you create when your business is defined as "electric power tools". You would employ armies of engineers (they may even become your core competency – the most senior of them may even run the business) and you would have a major research and development effort into electric motors, materials technology to improve the drill bits and the like.

If your business were defined as "holes" you might well have a marketing campaign that would not even mention the technical excellence of your products.

How about "Any hole, anywhere, anytime."

That suddenly turns you into a service business rather than a product business.

If that was how your business was defined I would suggest that you would outsource access to all the best technologies for making holes. Drills would not be a core competency. You would create powerful alliances with all those technology and tool providers.

I'm sure that in the foreseeable future it will become common place to use lasers to make perfect holes around the home and office (any hole, anywhere, anytime) without any fuss at all. Today lasers are already so effective and powerful that they can remove layers one molecule thick from your cornea. The price of lasers is falling at a similar rate to microprocessors. How long do you think it will be before these lasers are small and cheap enough to be sold as disposable DIY tools – and make the most perfect holes you have ever seen?

How about buying "a hole in a box".

I guess it would most likely be a six-pack of holes. A disposable laser pack containing six holes, 3 mm wide and 12 mm deep.

What about other new technologies such as ultrasound? The typical problem is that any business so focused on improving an existing technology (eg "power tools") may actually miss these new threats and opportunities simply because they fall outside the traditional focus of "what our business is!" These new innovations may even be seen as "competitive" – to be understood and fought against!

The moment the answer to the question "What is my business?" changes, these peripheral new technologies suddenly give you the opportunity to redefine your business. You might change from a "product focused" business to one focused on "relationships" or "solutions".

When you consider that almost any "product" business tends to become commoditized as it reaches maturity (characterized by increasing efficiency, more competitors and falling prices) the best business to be in is "relationships", "services" and "solutions". This is where the customer typically attaches high "value" and from which you can attract "profit" in the long term.

There are of course many businesses that have asked the "What is our business?" question and come up with a surprising answer. What should be interesting to us is that so few businesses have acted boldly on the answer.

Perhaps an even more telling question is

"What would we choose our future business to be?"

Given perfect choice, for most companies, it would not be an extrapolation of today's business. Given a clean sheet, given your experience and your knowledge of future markets, would you re-create in the future what you already have today?

Those who have acted radically in response to this question have frequently become widely recognized case studies. Think of global household names such as Nokia (previously a forest products company), and General Electric (a lumbering industrial age giant before Jack Welch turned its profit focus into financial services).

So, what do you choose
your future business to be?

Got it?

Now you're ready to think about Radical innovation.

To start with, you have to accept that
you'll need to understand

the future better than the past!

Radical innovation often succeeds because great entrepreneurs have a lucid anticipation of future markets.

It's always a "new generation" market out there. Whatever made you successful is by definition already a commodity.

How can you understand the future better than the past?

Over the past 15 years, working to help FutureWorld clients better understand the future, we have evolved a process that, like success, has many fathers. I call it Strategic Thinking and Strategic Action™.

The Traveller's Tale

A traveller encounters a wise old man in the desert and asks him directions to his destination. The old man looks up at the sky quizzically. He frowns. Then he contemplates the horizon and starts to speak. "Well…" he says, and then stops abruptly. He turns his attention to his feet. Dusty bare feet that have never known shoes. With the wisdom of ages he turns to look the desperate stranger in the eye. Hesitatingly he utters the traveller's worst fears: "If you want to get **there**, then you wouldn't start from **here**."

The principle behind this way of thinking is that in a market environment that is changing at break-neck speed, the worst place to start contemplating your future is from where you are now.

In a sense, if you want to get to the future,

the worst place to start

thinking about the future

is here, in the present.

You may recall the hoary old story of the lost traveller, as told opposite.

Every aspect of the present is in some way derived from the historic baggage of your past. All your past experiences, success and failure, have congealed into what makes you what you are today.

So, the first challenge is to separate your thinking about today, from your thinking about the future.

Drawing a thick black wiggly line between your thinking about the present and your thinking about the future is not as easy as it seems.

If you ask any team of managers how much time they think the top management team ought to be spending on creating the future rather than operating the present, the answer is always predictable: "More than they do today."

A straw poll we have frequently done with our clients typically throws up perceptions such as those shown on the following page.

Isn't it top management's job to create the future of the business? Doesn't the top team appoint middle management to operate the business for them?

PRESENT | **FUTURE**

Middle management perceptions of how much of their time top management spends on "strategy and creating the future", versus "operating the present"?

How much of their time do you think they **ought to be spending** on "the future"?

More than 50%

How much of their time do you think they **are spending** on "the future"?

10 to 30%

The amount of time that **is actually being spent** (based on an analysis of top management diaries).

Less than 10%

When we then analyze a top team's diary we usually find that they spend significantly less than 10 per cent on what is perceived to be their primary role in the business – creating the future.

Consider management behaviour during an average business day or business meeting. We delight in reporting actual numbers and extrapolating them into short-term plans. We talk about results and customer satisfaction ratings with passion. If a client call comes in complaining about some operational issue then the executive team jumps to it! We love it! It's where we feel most comfortable. We are all the business equivalent of action heroes.

The most creative of strategic thoughts **can be drowned by** the flow of operational crises.

It's almost as if the future isn't really all that important. Consider who should really be running the operations of the business. As an executive, didn't you hire a really top person to do that for you? Let them do it! Don't meddle. As an executive you should be focusing more than half your time, energy and wisdom on creating the future of your business.

You know you should. They expect it of you. So why does it not happen?

Years of working with top management teams has led me to one inescapable conclusion:

Contemplating the future is **the second most unnatural act that** you can ask the established executive **to perform.**

Somehow the here and now is so much more comfortable. We love to be seen to be doing something. Fixing a problem. But be careful.

Never confuse
activity with progress.
Especially when it comes to the future.

This dilemma seldom hits young businesses. In an upstart business you're completely focused on building the future business and there is very little current reality to intrude into your passionate dreams about the future. You won't reach this critical stage of the business life cycle until you become successful and your product and customer base grows.

In contrast, think about how most existing, mature businesses spend their average business day. It's almost completely focused on "our business". In fact it's primarily an internal view concerned with internal relationships, internal efficiencies, costs, targets, product sales, etc.

When we detect problems with meeting some of these targets or the well-oiled business machine is challenged by inputs from the outside ("customer problems", "crazy new competitors") we are prompted to look externally at the forces threatening the smooth running of the business machine. Typically these are only tended when the noise from outside gets unbearable for those on the inside.

Every now and then, when "environmental" factors threaten the business (eg changes in legislation, dropping of import barriers, changes in labour law or new technologies, etc) do we grudgingly take the time to consider their impact. Even so, most of this energy is focused on their current impact – reactive management.

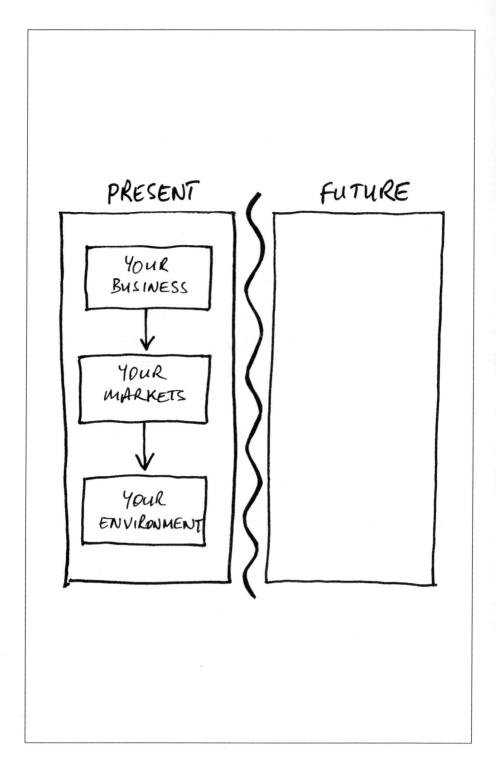

This is how most established businesses focus on their business – from the inside out.

How then can you create a balance between the focus on *today* and *the future*?

The trick is to build an artificial boundary between the present and the future, and focus the mind firmly on the future by constructing a vital and inspiring way to think about it. The diagram opposite represents that process at a fundamental level.

You have to actively "ring fence" the process of contemplating the future, turn it into a conscious skill and then make it an integral part of your on-going business thinking.

At some point in this process most executive teams have come to the startling but obvious conclusion that you cannot think about the future of your business in the same way that you react to the present.

While you may run your business on a day-to-day basis primarily from the inside out, you can only design your future business from the outside in.

The starting point for thinking about the future of your business is not your current business. The best place to start is the future environment. This may be counter-intuitive and it certainly may not appear to fast-track us to a vision for the future, but in a fast-changing marketplace it's the only place to start – by understanding the environment of the marketplace of the future.

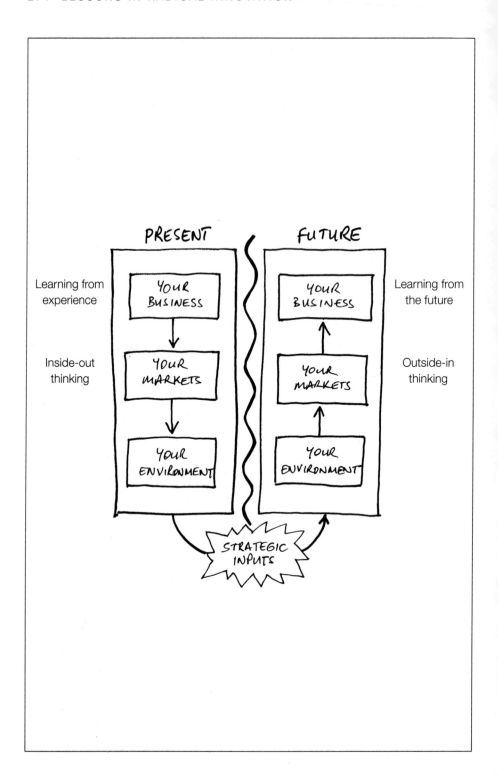

Strategic Inputs are the first step in a process we call "Learning from the Future". This is the antithesis of the inside-out way of understanding our existing business – this is ouside-in thinking.

In this warp-speed world it is simply not enough to learn from experience – you must learn from the future. Let's see how it works in practice.

At first look you might say it's impossible to learn from the future. How can you know what the future will be?

Despite the radical changes going on all around there are some key "rules of the game" that will help us identify the forces that will prove instrumental in shaping our future environment. Also, there are some "key uncertainties" that could cause the future environment to shape up into two or more possible scenarios.

Then there are those "wild cards" – unlikely but powerful events that could destroy the most basic of our assumptions.

technologies that will:
change production processes
change consumer behaviour
open new markets
increase life span
dramatically cut costs of food, drugs, etc

political and regulatory actions that will:
change employment practices
raise operating costs
open markets to competition

social trends that will:
create pressure on global companies
build resistance to global brands
give preference to organic and "green" products
cause consumers to exercise their individual and group power

This is where our series of Strategic Inputs comes in. We establish with our clients what they expect to be the key factors that will shape their business environment in the future. A typical list of these is shown opposite.

The list can be almost endless. It should be focused on your business priorities, and based on answers to the following questions:

What is it about the future that will create positive or negative changes for business?

What are those things we know that we don't know enough about?

What are those things we don't know that we don't know about?

(This dilemma is best answered by staying close to your markets and by the youngest, brightest people in your business)

We then line up top experts and visionaries to explore each of these issues in a series of Strategic Inputs – powerful explorative presentations followed by "So what?" debates. We ask: "What if what we have just heard does happen? What will be the implications for markets? What new opportunities will be created? What will customers 'value'? What will be the implications for our business in the future?"

Our experts or "gurus" are all briefed to discuss their area of speciality in a *future perfect* tense. (For more on this approach read Stan Davis' classic book *FuturePerfect*.)

The FutureWorld
Network of Gurus…
designing the future

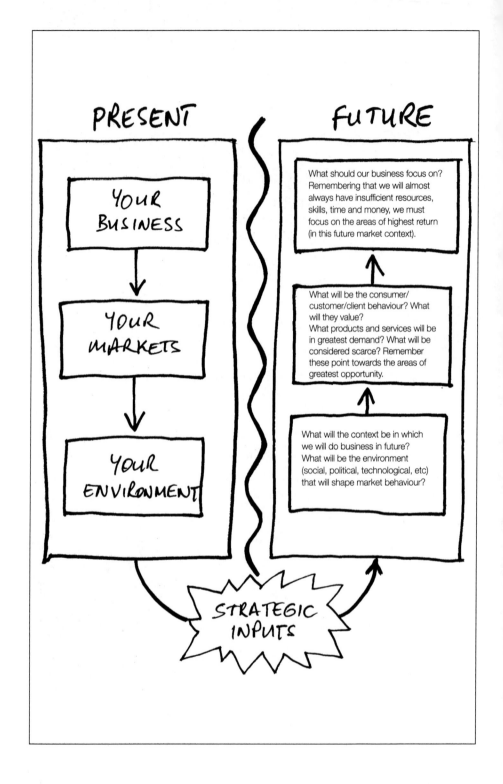

In each of their areas of speciality we begin to
imagine the future as if
it has already happened.

Imagining the future is really a three-step process as shown opposite.

It's only when you understand the future market context that you can design your desired role within it. And if you have the chance to design your future, why design anything less than your ideal future?

Detail is important in both the *understand* and *design* phase. What are we doing? What cars are we driving? How are consumers behaving? Who are our competitors? You have to be able to feel and touch the future.

What started out as a process of Divergent Thinking, based on a challenging series of Strategic Inputs, now turns into a process of Convergent Thinking working towards a series of Strategic Actions.

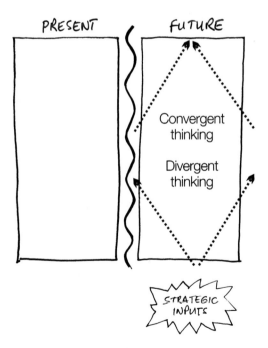

Having debated all the possibilities in the environment, markets and business opportunities, we now have to choose a future for our business.

This is a debate and the outcome is anything but certain. The trick is to consider all the different views of the future, no matter how divergent. We literally have to thrash it out.

If everyone agrees – you know you're on the wrong track. Someone's not thinking clearly. Someone's missed the radical opportunity.

The scary thing is that at this stage, where you are contemplating a really radical opportunity, all the tried and trusted analytical approaches do not help a jot. Market research is useless if the markets don't yet exist. It is folly to ask consumers about radical future products that they cannot even imagine. You'll remember what happened when Sony asked consumers if they had a need for the Walkman, or when early PC pioneers tried to encourage people to think about computers at home. Whatever would we do with them?

However, perfect choice about the future still means that the group has to converge around one ideal future as the basis for their thinking.

What one vision for this business can we all feel united and passionate about?

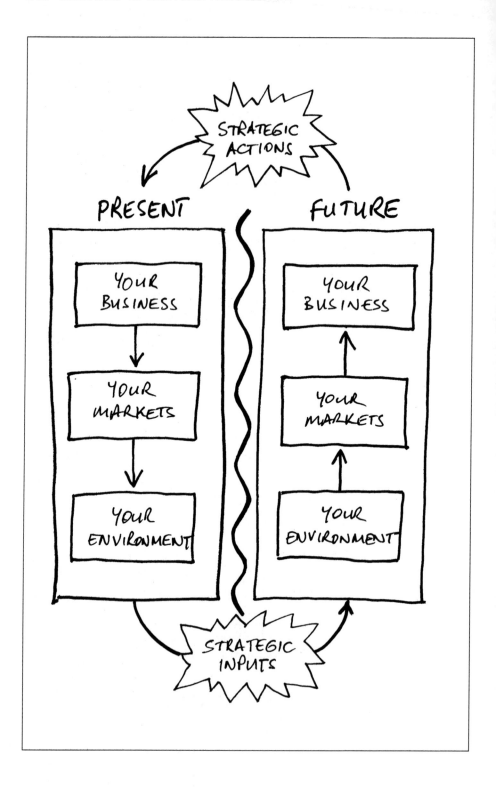

Once we have developed our passionate vision for the future, we need to plant our feet firmly in this future and look back from whence we came: "Gee, isn't this 'future' great. I'm really proud to be a part of this thriving business. But, looking back five years, how did we ever get here? What were the Strategic Actions we took back then to create this reality?"

You see, Strategic Actions are never

actions we take in the future.
Strategic Actions are those we

take today,
to create our ideal future.

This process does more than define the gap between our future reality and the current reality of the past. It shows us how we bridged the gap. It helps us identify the imperative for Strategic Actions.

It's so much easier and more effective to do this thinking in a future perfect tense. No one can argue that it can't be done. It has been done and that's all there is to it. Now, doesn't it feel great?

Do not take this shortcut to your future!

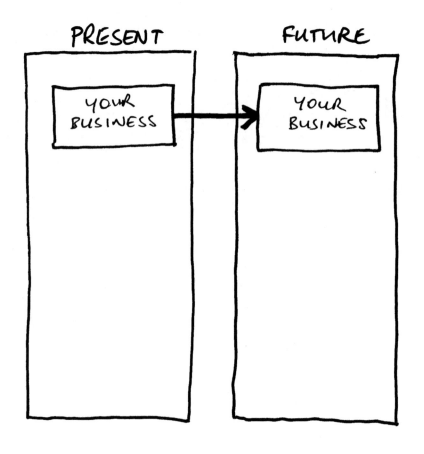

This is not to say that the real future does not have various scenarios. The scenario planning process recognizes that there are a number of possible future scenarios for the environment, markets and of course for your business. The whole field of scenario planning is best handled using other publicly available sources. In practice, in my work with FutureWorld and their clients, I have found the need to create a powerful pragmatic approach to short circuit the time-consuming processes typically associated with scenario planning.

We call our approach "Strategic Action Scenarios™" and it allows an executive team to see and explore the inter-relationships of the various factors influencing the future in an extremely graphical way. One of the outputs of this process can typically be a 3D structure like this one below.

Strategic Action Scenarios ™

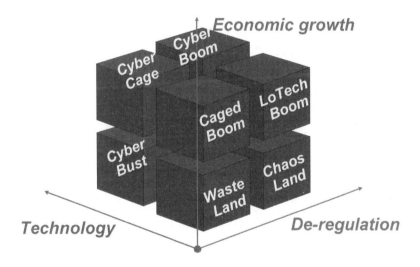

This example creates eight possible future scenarios from which the team can choose one "scenario of choice" to serve as the basis for Strategic Thinking.

Look at the diagram opposite. Whatever you do, do not try to contemplate your future this way!

In my experience, when we try to create a view of the future by extrapolating from our past success and where we are today, we fall horribly short of the ideal.

We are encumbered by all our own current paradigms of the future. We know why things won't work and justify to ourselves that the really difficult stuff is really not worth the effort. Just think of all the people you will have to win over. Just think of all the politics. Let's just go for something a little more modest.

Allow me to paraphrase Charles Handy who explained the dilemma brilliantly:

"We are walking backwards into the future, with our eyes firmly fixed on our past achievements."

We are literally blinded by the past.

As individuals and as a business we must turn around and look the future squarely in the face! Resist the temptation of romantic dreams about the way things were and what made us so successful in the past.

In order to innovate radically, you must learn to

learn from the future!

We have found that Strategic Thinking and Strategic Action™ is a pragmatic process for creating the foundations for radical innovation.

Try it yourself.

This can be a fully inclusive process in which all the bright young things in your business can participate. It's a process which can also give you the opportunity to bring your business partners, suppliers and customers actively into the process of choosing your future.

With Strategic Thinking and Strategic Action™ you can build an idealized view of your future that will create a powerful context for radical innovation and the thought leadership you need to harness the bright stuff in your business. You too can choose your future, together.

And why stop after doing it within your business? Try it with your family!

evolutionary	radical
Telephone	Mobile phone
Banks	Non-banks
Retail	e-tail
Transport	Logistics
Education	Learning
Hardware/software	Solutions
Chemical	Biotech
Pharmaceutical	Life sciences
Computer software	The software of living things
Manufacturing physical stuff	Networking information

Remember, you are what you do.

If the preceding chapters have taught us anything, it is that radical innovation powerfully lays the foundations for new markets and future growth.

Just check out these industries listed opposite, their attitudes to innovation, and consider which you believe will thrive in the new global context. While there are always exceptions to the rule, I've taken the opportunity to categorize these industries in the table opposite.

Just think about how the mobile phone industry has innovated customers away from the traditional telephone industries – all in less than a decade! That's radical innovation at many levels.

In the USA, for years now, the primary innovators in banking services have not been the banks. Almost every type of company has muscled into their turf – from car manufacturers and retailers to electricity companies. Some say that more than 90 per cent of new banking services now come from non-banks.

In retailing, the realization has dawned that competition is no longer between products (they're commoditized and available through everyone) but between business models. Many retailers are turning large chunks of their business into e-tail operations. A merger between a WalMart and an Amazon.com may still be a win–win deal for both parties.

Hardware and software companies, always the darlings of investors in the first half of the industry life cycle, are turning to solutions and services business to regain lost profitability. They are turning to what the market-place now sees as "value". IBM, having made that decision in the early 1990s, clearly has a massive first mover advantage here.

Life sciences and biotech firms are the radical innovators today and many traditional players in chemicals and pharmaceuticals are transforming their conglomerates to align them with the new opportunities for innovation and growth. As these industries discover the power of the "software of living things" and further explore the possibilities of the human, animal and plant genomes, they will become the most dramatic growth industry of the 21st Century. For more on these developments read my previous book, *Ten Lessons from the Future.*

Look for the telltale signs of evolutionary innovation, evolution focused on products and services in your own business and in your markets.

Use the Creative Destruction matrix in Chapter 1 to create an innovation profile for your business.

Ask yourself: Which of the above industries would I rather be a part of? The answer depends on your personal appetite for risk!

Ask yourself: Which industries will have the biggest growth in the long term? Which industries would I invest in for the long term?

If you chose evolutionary innovation...
After 600 million years of evolutionary innovation...
...you would still be an echinoderm.
In a dark swamp of a market somewhere.
Nobody would know you anymore.
Alive but not thriving.

However, if you chose radical innovation...
After just a few years you could become...
...a dominant new species,
...the Tiger Woods of your industry,
or one of *Fortune*'s Top Companies!
If you did achieve this...how would you feel?

Energized? Yes. Fulfilled? Certainly. Resonant? You'd feel it! Exhausted? Without doubt!

But, most of all, you'd probably feel Proud!

And, ultimately, isn't that exactly what radical success is all about?

At the heart of these lessons in
radical innovation are
bold visionary individuals
who are proud of what they've created.

Radical innovation is driven through the "unreasonable" behaviour of individuals, typically those who end up becoming the heroes of the revolution.

Remember...without personal passion,
the cows of radical innovation don't calve!

MY CANVAS OF POSSIBILITIES

Lessons learnt

Step 1:
Nail down what you think you are today!

Step 2:
Consider the changing context of your future – apply divergent thinking to the environmental and market factors driving future customer needs and behaviour

Step 3:
Understand your possible futures so you can touch and feel the options – apply convergent thinking around a preferred future

Step 4:
Choose your ideal future and feel how it feels

Step 5:
From your future perspective, ask – how did we get here? Identify the strategic actions you took to get to your ideal future

Step 6:
Step back into today and kick off those essential strategic actions – do it now!

Step 7:
Create your future

Step 8:
Enjoy it and you'll thrive in it!